OUR MONEY NARRATIVE AND THE IMPACTS ON OUR FINANCIAL WELLNESS

The "Thing$" We Don't Talk About

HEATHER COLEMAN

Lucky Book Publishing

"Education is a superpower and if we take that mindset to our financial wellness, it is life-changing."

- Heather Coleman

MY GIFT TO YOU

I am so glad you're here!

As my Gift to you, get FREE Access to the Audiobook of Our Money Narrative and other Free Book Bonuses by scanning the QR Code below or visiting www.heathercoleman.ca

WHAT I HOPE TO BRING BY SHARING THIS BOOK

Money is a silent struggle for many people. I want to share my passion for financial literacy and financial wellness with the world. I am hoping through this journey you will be able to take one or more of the following things away:

- Understand that money issues can be resolved

- You are not alone in your money narrative

- You have the power to make the necessary changes

- Understanding your money narrative can be one way to help increase your overall financial wellbeing

- Feeling empowered to make financial wellness a priority starts with you

- Enough with the silence - let's start talking about money

- Stop tripping over yourself when it comes to your cash!

I dedicate this book to my two little pickles (Tenley & Camryn) who I hope continue to shine bright everyday.

Thank you to my tribe for always supporting me - Mom, Tina, Aunty Baby, Stephy, my work wife NJ and my Spiderman.

For more information about services available to help you head to www.heathercoleman.ca

TABLE OF CONTENTS

Chapter 7

FOREWORD BY KEVIN COCHRAN – THE BEGINNING OF ENRICHED ACADEMY

My name is Kevin Cochran, and I am one of the co-founders of Enriched Academy, which we started in the early 2000s. It all started with my buddy, Jay Seabrook, CoFounder, and me going around doing high school talks in Personal Finance because, to be honest, we were not taught about money growing up.

I grew up in Toronto, Ontario and went to Don Mills Collegiate High School which was one of the biggest schools in the area. After finishing high school, I did not continue on to College or University because, one, they didn't let me in, and, two, I was not quite sure what I even wanted to do. So, after working a bunch of random jobs, the one consistent thing I learned was that I did not know much about the one thing all those random jobs had in common, MONEY.

I had accumulated about $20,000 in credit card debt, including my first car purchase. Here is a very early piece of advice: do not buy your first car on a credit card. As I mentioned, I was not the smartest in school, so looking at 19% interest on a credit card statement meant nothing to me.

After making some serious money mistakes, I decided there had to be a better way. So, I worked my butt off to pay off that debt and when I started working for Richard Robbins in my early 20s, I was able to learn and see the importance of knowing where to put your money and how to live to ensure that you were not overleveraging.

The funny thing was when we started teaching this stuff, we put a lot (and I mean A LOT) of students to sleep. If you have ever spoken to a bunch of high school kids, you know that they are one tough audience. They will not be afraid to fall asleep, boo at you, or even throw things. But after we started making some serious blunders, we were finally able to get the message right. We received a phone call from this one kid's dad to let us know that whatever we said that day made strides. She wanted to return all her Christmas gifts, take the money and start investing to take advantage of compounding interest.

This led Jay and I to start building Enriched Academy with our DVD kit that brought us to the Dragon's Den, a Canadian show you might also recognize as Shark

Tank, in which entrepreneurs can pitch their ideas to successful business people. Hint: we were successful in getting a deal, but it did not come easy. We auditioned in Toronto and were turned down. That's right. However, Jay and I have one thing in common, we do not give up easily. This trait is a large part of the character and essence which makes up Enriched Academy. So, we hopped on a flight to Vancouver and showed up at the casting call the next day. The team was impressed by this and let us audition. That one opportunity/decision really did open the door for us as we were able to secure a deal with Jim Treliving (for those of you living under a rock, the owner of Boston Pizza and Mr. Lube) and Bruce Croxon, who is best known for founding Lavalife among other businesses.

While Enriched Academy has significantly grown from those days of selling DVD kits on how to teach your kids about money to DragonBanks, I am proud to see that we are helping hundreds of thousands of Canadians through our ongoing programming online through our Education, Coaching, and Associations/Corporations divisions.

Ultimately, the whole concept behind Enriched Academy comes down to helping the average person learn about money in a place with no shame, no bullshit (sorry Heather – had to throw one curse word in here), and with no bias.

If anyone gets to know Heather, she is one firecracker who we brought on in 2021. I have come to know many people over the years in my role as one of the owners of Dominion Lending Centre, travelling across the country and inspiring Canadians to make that commitment to themselves to make money a priority, and I can honestly say, this girl is passionate.

I believe in being genuinely you, and Heather is just that. When she said she wanted to embark on a journey to write this book to share with the world the passion for financial literacy we helped spark, I could not have been more supportive. If you want to commit yourself to making financial wellness a priority, this is one thing you won't regret.

CHAPTER 1
INTRODUCTION

"We all show up to work every day for the same reason
but why? It's because we love our jobs right?
Not exactly, it's Money."
– Heather Coleman

The History Behind the Story

We know that money makes the world go round, but
we do not talk about it. So, what's the problem with
that? We are conditioned to avoid one topic that literally
impacts all of us every day. We know talking about the
hard stuff can be difficult – but have you ever stopped
to think to yourself, why is it that we do not talk about
money? Why is it that I was never taught to budget, save,
invest, get out of debt etc., but I was taught algebra and
learn all the different types of triangles – which, by the
way, looking at my desk I see an isosceles – wait or is
right-angled – I do not even know anymore, and that's
the problem here. Obviously, those of us who decided
to use geometry in our careers and life may have better

uses for the different types of triangles and why they matter. However, the average person, like you and me, does not.

So, let's break that cycle. Let's start talking about the thing we were told not to talk about: MONEY. Regardless, if you have some, have none, think about it all the time, stress about it, or are motivated by it, this book will begin to talk about Financial Wellness from a different perspective than has ever been done: a real, person to person conversation. No real advice on exactly what you should be doing with it, because let's get real, we all have our own goals, ambitions, holdbacks, and impacts that will ultimately change the trajectory of what we do with our money, but let's talk about the fundamentals of why financial wellness matters, why having a passion for it will help change your money narratives, and add some funny stories about money that will hopefully be relatable and help you on your path to making financial decisions through a lens of taking action.

To get started, here is a little bit about me. I am the youngest of four girls in my family. Yes, you read that right, four girls. Do not feel bad for my father though, I believe karma gifted him with some very strong-willed, independent women for a reason.

I grew up in a single-income household, one that was a bit unorthodox because it was my mother who was the breadwinner as a legal assistant, whereas my father was on disability. So, I got to witness a mother trying to balance four girls, three of whom were in competitive sports, trying to buy groceries that were meant to last until her next paycheque. This resulted in a box of Joe Louis cakes being divided into two each for the entire 14-day period. When you ate them was ultimately up to you, but we learned that if you divided them into quarters and shared them with your siblings, having that delicious treat, or a piece of it, once per day was better than nothing.

In our house, having a single income led to becoming accustomed to a simple and humble lifestyle. One that led to shared Christmas presents, hand-me-downs, and new shoes only at the beginning of school when the baby bonus cheque came in. All these small things impacted my money narrative. And this led me to my passion for finances when I started my own dog-walking business at the age of nine. The thought of having my own money to buy my things such as penny candies that I did not have to share with my siblings may have had a significant impact here.

This passion grew when I started my first job at 12. I was a cashier at Burger King. A little blonde-haired "sasspants," who convinced the hiring manager that I wanted to work as a cashier because I like people, and they like me. I was too young to touch the fryers for insurance purposes, but the manager liked the "cut of my jib" or whatever that statement is and gave me the opportunity to talk to people for a living. Yes, maybe this was a bit of foreshadowing for my career to date, but I will go into that story in another book.

My stepdad was a teacher through and through,(for those who know Bucky you know what I mean), and when I brought home my first paycheque of a whooping $180, he took me to cash the cheque and proceeded to take 50% of my earnings. Wait a minute, I know what you are thinking, why is giving my money away to my dad a financially literate decision? Isn't giving your money away a bad thing? Why yes, yes, it is. But stay with me here for a minute.

So, my dad started a wonderful spreadsheet on his Macintosh desktop, where he tallied up my total paycheque, the amount I kept for fun Heather, and the 50% I gave him for my savings. He took that money and put it into a GIC locked away for six months. I never asked what a GIC was or why he wanted 50% of the money. I just listened to him at the time, hoping he would have my best interest at heart. What I did not realize then, which I do now, was that he was trying to teach me financial literacy. He was trying to pass on what he knew based on what his parents had taught him.

Because let's get real, that is how you used to learn. You had parents who taught you what they knew, assuming what they knew was decent, OR you go to the school of hard knocks and learn what not to do by making a couple of mistakes. Like my first credit card. It was actually my second that was the true problem though.

My stepdad took me to get my first credit card at the age of 18. We went to the bank and requested a $500 limit credit card to get me going. He advised me to start using that credit card for everything and to pay it off in full every month. We broke down how much money I was earning and saving and how, if I were to use the credit card before cash, I would be doing two things:

i.   building my credit to be able to buy a home someday and

ii. ensuring that I was learning to be diligent with the amount of money I was spending per month.

I realize now the time and effort my stepdad was putting into trying to teach me the basics of money management would stick with me later in life. However, sometimes, we get external influences.

I was attending a concert in my hometown of Ottawa, and they were giving away Ottawa Senators blankets for anyone who applied for a credit card. There was a cute boy that I knew from junior high school who was working that stand. So, of course, I wanted to help a friend out by allowing him to hit his quota in credit card applications for the day, and to be honest, I may have been thinking that a date would be coming as well.

It was a couple of weeks later that I got approved for an $800 limit credit card. Yeah, me. The only problem is that I failed to share the news with my financial instructor because the thought of applying for a credit card due to a cute boy working the desk may not have gone over well with my stepdad. Lo and behold, I now had two credit cards. One I was using diligently and the other just sitting there, in my bedside table drawer waiting for that boy to call me for a date. Well, the boy never called, and that credit card did not sit in that bedside table drawer for long.

My sister had moved to Vancouver and had asked me to come for a visit before starting university in the fall. Given the amount of savings I had accumulated, I had requested my parents use a portion of that to pay for my flight so I could have some adventures before heading to university to start my studies. Even though my stepdad did not quite agree with dipping into the savings, the argument that I would work extra shifts to pay back what I borrowed from myself upon my return led him to believe that my commitment and diligence to date with my money habits would lead me in the right direction. And he begrudgingly agreed. Well, he probably should have pushed back harder because what did I do on that trip without my money coach present? I spent every penny on my first credit card, and that lonely card that sat in my bedside table was also maxed out.

It took less than two weeks to completely blow up every good money habit I had built up to date. And what did I have to show for it? I had a lot of good laughs, some good drinks and eats, good company, a couple of headaches, sunburns, and retail therapy purchases.

When I came home, I had to explain to my stepdad that I needed the rest of my savings to pay for my maxed-out credit cards. And his answer? NOPE. You got yourself into this mess by overleveraging yourself, and using your savings allotted for long-term planning is not the solution. You have 30 days to work extra shifts, to make the extra money back PLUS the savings amount you promised to pay back. And why did he do this? Because he was trying to build the resilience muscle in me to pay myself first and to instill the knowledge that using your savings account is not the solution for silly money mistakes. If you cannot afford to purchase things you bought on your credit card, then you are not using your credit card appropriately, and as such your future self should not be punished because of your desire to fulfill a need today.

The good news, I was able to make the extra money to pay off both of those credit cards, but I was not able to add the extra money back into my savings account. I share this story for a couple of reasons, one being that most of us have a similar story. Some people though continue not to earn extra income but have to live with the habits of overleveraging themselves and getting dinged with high-interest payments. Because credit cards easily help you spend money quickly, regardless of whether you have the income or budget to pay it back. Secondly, if you do not have a version of this story to relate to, I am sure you have some stories of your own that impact your money narrative. Moments that define you and your money habits, which, if you stop and reflect on today, you can start to see their impact on you and the decisions you make in your money life every day. Reflect on those for a moment.

What was the one story that stuck out to you when you started making money a priority for yourself? Or starting to view money as difficult and a sore spot? Or viewing money as something you need, want, and would solve all your problems?

We have all been impacted by our money decisions to date, whether these are good, bad, or ugly. It really does not matter because the best part about financial wellness is that where you are today or how money impacted you in the past does not have to be forever. The cool thing is you can learn to redefine your future with your money narrative and learn to take some easy steps to make financial wellness a priority.

Listen, I get it, money can bring out some of the worst in people, and I have experienced my fair share of witnessing nastiness when it comes to money. From my biological father taking the full amount of insurance money awarded to our family because of an accidental house fire, which left my mother to furnish an entire house for four girls with less than $20,000, to my stepsister making my early-onset dementia grandmother change her will the day after my stepdad died to make her the sole person to inherit her "fortune" – which was a whopping $80,000. And to an ex-husband who had taken $200,000 from our joint line of credit, without my knowledge or consent, less than two months after our separation. This one made me vomit and cry instantly. So, money struggles are real.

I did not grow up with a passion for personal finance. I grew up in an average household, with parents who took the time to pass on what they knew and helped me recognize that if you take a little bit of time to care about this topic, it really can be life-changing when it comes to your future.

This book is designed to start a conversation with you about your money narrative. It provides a non-judgemental approach to discussing money, offers fundamental perspectives about it, and addresses a core learning gap that none of us had the opportunity to master in our education. Even for those of us who feel that we have a good grip on our money – sometimes life throws curveballs. And money is generally always impacted by those curveballs. So regardless of where you are in your money journey, hopefully, this book brings you some inspiration to make your financial wellness a priority.

This book will include some real-life stories that will be used throughout the book. I am a firm believer that sharing stories and some good laughs is a great way to learn. No one really needs more shame when it comes to money, so let's have some laughs as we move to helping everyone improve their money narratives.

Many of these stories come from Enriched Academy, and I am truly thankful to Jay, Kevin and Todd for giving me the creative freedom to take their brainchild and turn it into a read for many others to enjoy. Their passion for bringing Financial Literacy across Canada for the average Canadian, in a way that has not been done before, is not only inspiring but also makes me proud every day to be a part of something that matters. I also need to credit Kevin McCarthy, Alanna Abramsky, Arian Beyzaei, Jay Tost, Amy Martin, Sonya Fox, Natalie Joy Quesnel, Kate Antic, Mama Susan, Mama Renee and the rest of the team at EA for continuing to share the passion of bringing such an important topic to many others daily. You have been my work family away from my family and I am deeply thankful to have had the privilege of working with such awesome folks.

Key Takeaways

- Be sure to keep an open mind while reading this book. There are many reflection questions throughout for you to stop, pause, and take the time to really dig in.

- You can use the end of each chapter to enter your answers, the blank pages at the end, or request a copy of the accompanying workbook at www.heathercoleman.ca

- Be mindful that your narratives can change overtime. Coming back to certain chapters at a later point is a good practice to commit to and is an easy task to put into your calendar now as a reminder.

Questions for you to think about before we get started

1. Do you have any money stories from your childhood that you recall?

2. Do you have any misconceptions about money that you can name before we get started?

3. Do you have any preconceived notions about your own money narrative?

CHAPTER 2
MONEY MYTHS PART 1

"Only two people can have your money,
you or somebody else."
- Kevin Cochran

There are a lot of misconceptions about money. Being aware of the money myths and how they impact your narratives is important.

In this section, let's talk about SEX, baby – wait, no. MONEY. That's a great song though.

If we are conditioned never to talk about money, how can we demystify it?. We are going to start by getting your commitment to being real with yourself and beginning to talk about money. Start being comfortable with the uncomfortable.

I want you to use this section to start highlighting opportunities to think about how money myths impact you. Consider how you can overcome these myths or how to address them in your day-to-day life. I want you to be more mindful of the impacts these myths have on you and your money narrative.

Myth # 1 – You Need Money to Make Money

Well, this one is kind of true because if you do not have any income coming in, it will be difficult to manage it and learn to grow it. So, we will talk about this one in the context of the drive to have more and more and MORE.

Let's look back at this concept. Does anyone remember the old statement "Keeping up with the Joneses"? The reference was from a comic strip originally from 1913, in which one family, the McGinnis', tried to keep up with their neighbours' social status. The author, Arthur Pop Momand, highlighted the overconsumption mindset that had started to develop within domestic America. The Joneses would get a new "toy," furniture, or other commodity, which led to the McGinnis' trying to find ways to compete or keep up with them. Now the basics of this premise are still true today. However, do you find that some pieces of this concept do not fit anymore?

Why do I say this? Because our overconsumption habits have grown from the simple Joneses to the Kardashian levels. We find ourselves watching TV shows or YouTube series with basic families exploding into fame and fortune with extreme lifestyles and money. However, the interesting thing is some of these extreme "millionaires" have nothing to show for it after the money starts coming in.

Where do we see this the most often? Professional athletes. We had the pleasure of interviewing Chris Pronger, former National Hockey League (NHL) legend who shared that he knows so many of his former colleagues who have nothing to show for their previous significant incomes. He took to Twitter and said "I played 20 years in the NHL. I was one of the highest earning NHL players of all time. And friends with many other pro athletes. My guess is more than 50% of pro athletes have financial issues in retirement." Why is this? Did they have a hard time keeping up with their earnings? Some would argue yes because they only make peak dollars for a couple of years in their career. However, regardless of the amount of income they were making, if they had no skills to manage it, then poor money mistakes would continue.

Most of the time, they develop spending habits based on the highest earnings they make. This means that as soon as that money stops coming in, they do not adjust their spending habits. So, what happens? Like the average person, we get ourselves into overspending and overleveraging. This results in higher debt levels or impacts on our future savings.

NHL players are not the only ones impacted. Major League Baseball (MLB) players are some of the highest-paid athletes of all time, and statistics show that they go bankrupt four times the national average.

National Basketball Association (NBA) players are not hard up when it comes to earning money either, with an average salary of 9.6 million per year. However, 60% of NBA players go into financial distress within five years of retirement. Why is this? Do they have a hard time making money? No.

The issue here comes down to the fact that they were not taught how to manage it. They were taught how to play their sport. They were taught to be experts in their field. They were not taught what to do with the copious amount of money coming their way in a very short period of time. They were not taught to think beyond their current contract. They were not taught to think about the financial impacts that earning that much money will have on them today versus tomorrow.

I know what some of you are thinking, "Why should I feel bad for them? They made some poor choices. But I'm sure they got to live a lifestyle that I can only dream about." Maybe you are right in your position on that. We should not feel bad for these pro-athletes who are making millions of dollars in a year. But I only highlight these examples to demonstrate that it does not matter how much money you make - if you do not know how to manage that money, statistics show that you are going to end up in financial distress.

Let's look at the lottery and the winners there. How many times have you said to yourself, "If I only win the lottery, my life would be changed." Now, I do not want to shame you for saying that. Jeez, some of the smartest people I know with their money sometimes buy lottery tickets, play poker, or attend a casino for a night out with friends. It's all good to have fun and have some experiences. However, too many people are relying on this as their saving grace from financial worries.

When you start digging into the statistics around winning the lottery though, some statistics state that 70% of lottery winners go bankrupt. 70%!!! Now, other stats say that the number is closer to 1/3 going bankrupt. No matter what the real number is, it is astoundingly high. The big lump sum of money will more than likely be mismanaged if you do not take the time to learn how to maximize it.

I met a man at a session I was training at in Iqaluit, Nunavut in 2023. He shared with me that he and his wife had won the lottery a year prior. However, he kept the money sitting in his chequing account because he was so scared to make a mistake. He was petrified of spending it, not spending it, or doing something with it that it would vanish away. I remember thinking to myself - the bank must love you. Keeping over 1 million of cash in your basic account, making no money at all. I did share with him that this approach was better than blowing through it but highly recommended that he comes up with a bit of a better strategy for it (do not worry - we will talk about this in chapter 6.)

So, what I want you to think about now is the fact that money does not discriminate. Everyone has the opportunity to make it. How much you make and the availability to obtain it based on your history, gender, culture etc. could be impacted by discrimination, but money itself does not. Everyone requires it to survive nowadays. In modern history, in this global economy, regardless of whether you come from a diverse background, if you do not know how to manage money, there is a very big chance you are going to suffer financial stress.

I spent more than two years researching this. More particularly, the impacts that financial stress has on employees. Here is what I found: regardless of income level, financial stress impacts all of us. So, whether it is the new recruit just starting out or the senior CEO making six or seven figures, the feelings are the same.

According to the Financial Consumer Agency of Canada, 42% of Canadians admitted to being impacted by financial stress. That impact results in a minimum of 3.5 hours per week lost in productivity.

Therefore, our ability to make money in the workplace is also impacted by the very financial stress we are dealing with while making it. Yes, I know that is a weird concept to wrap your head around. However, the key point I am trying to make is that the myth of "I need more money to solve my problems" is fundamentally wrong.

You need to adjust your mindset to focus on building muscle and the skills regarding how to maximize managing your money. Like learning a new language or a new hobby, you must commit to a new way of thinking about the skill you are developing.

Kevin Cochran, co-founder of Enriched Academy, always uses the analogy about going to the gym. Imagine you want to curl 100 lbs. You do not jump straight to pulling 100 lb dumbbells and curling. WHY? Because you are going to hurt yourself. You need to build up the proper form and start with a lower weight. Once you get the proper form and movements, your muscles begin to grow. So, you either add more repetitions to the form to ensure you are ready to move up to some more weight. Then you add more and more. Ensuring that all the way along, the fundamental form and proper finesse are being maintained. Because if it is not, guess what? You will drop some weight to ensure you do not hurt yourself.

Now, this is where you need to think about your money narrative.

Self-Reflection Questions

1. How many times have you asked for a raise?
2. How many times have you job-shopped for some extra income?
3. Have you considered getting a side hustle to earn more?

These concepts and questions all stem around the same myth, you think you need more money because you do not have enough coming in. In some cases, the truth is that you may not have enough income.

You could be in a position where the amount of money you make is not funding your current lifestyle. However, before jumping to this conclusion – again ask yourself, do you have the skills and are doing the steps to ensure that you are maximizing the amount you have coming in? If your answer is YES, then great, maybe finding ways to earn more will be your focus. However, a large part of my training and research says that your answer will be NO. Therefore, we will discuss some of these strategies in subsequent chapters, but for now, I want you to reflect on how the thought of more money impacts your narrative.

Myth # 2 – It Is Too Difficult

Money can be difficult as with anything else. However, your mindset here is what matters. Have you ever heard about the concept of positive affirmations? According to WebMD, "Positive affirmations are made up of phrases that you can say aloud to yourself or in your head. You can also write them down and make sure they're always visible. Positive affirmations are meant to help build you up and improve your confidence, even when things are difficult." Start your day by saying something like "I can do this," "I am beautiful," "I am strong," or "I am brave." When you hear it over and over, you start to believe it.

Now think about the affirmations or narratives you have concerning your money. Many of us take it down the road of saying, "This is too difficult," "I do not understand," or "This is too much for me." So, what do you think will happen? It will continue to influence your ability to think differently because you are conditioned to only hear those statements and start believing them to be true.

I want you to reflect on your money narrative here.

MONEY NARRATIVE REFLECTION

1. Do you find yourself speaking negatively or positively about your money situation?

2. Do you surround yourself with those who are positive money characters? Or negative?

3. When you are doing a money task – what is your mood? Positive, negative, indifferent?

These are important to start recognizing your patterns.

Now think about why people may find the concept of money difficult. Sometimes it simply comes down to the fact that some people are not numbers people. I understand that too. Math is a hard concept for many people to wrap their heads around. I will even admit that multiplying numbers beyond nine and no longer being able to rely on using my finger trick gets me to scratch my head. Good thing I do not need to recite math to understand money and this myth. Why? Because there are amazing tools such as calculators and spreadsheets that do that work for me. Thank goodness. Ask Todd, the CEO of Enriched Academy, how often he would have to ensure my basic addition of the number of people in a program was accurate. More than I would like to admit because if I did it off the top of my head,

I would sometimes miss an entire column. But once I transposed those into an Excel or calculator – BAM, my number world was so much better. Thank you for your patience, Todd.

I want you to get out of your way for this myth and look at some simple examples for removing the barriers to comprehension.

Enriched Academy has experience with some great, inspiring people, and I am excited to share one story in this section to demonstrate that money is simply a language you need to learn.

I will introduce Arian Beyzaei, who I like to refer to as the first Enriched Kid. At 16, Arian was filled with the excitement that comes with the promise of something big. A friend's grandfather, a man Arian admired for his wealth and wisdom, had just told him about a new company he was investing in. "You should put your money in," he said with the confidence of someone who had seen it all. The man's success was undeniable, and Arian, eager to start building his future, jumped at the chance. He scraped together every dollar he had saved – $5,000 earned from years of odd jobs, birthdays, and careful saving – and asked his mom to help him open an account. This was it; he thought. This was how people became rich.

For the next two weeks, Arian could not help but picture his future. He checked the stock daily, imagining what he'd do with the money once it grew. Maybe he'd buy his first car or reinvest and watch it keep growing. The possibilities seemed endless. But then, just as quickly as it had started, everything fell apart. The company went bankrupt.

In one devastating moment, Arian lost everything. His entire savings, gone in an instant. The $5,000 he had worked so hard for vanished, leaving him with nothing but a sinking feeling of regret and disbelief. How did this happen? How had it all disappeared so fast? The sting of losing his hard-earned money was unbearable, but even more painful was the realization that his dream of instant wealth had been just that, a dream.

Most people would have walked away, defeated, but not Arian. The loss was a hard blow for a young kid, but instead of giving up, he used it as fuel. That failure became his first real lesson in investing. He realized he could not rely on luck or the advice of others without fully understanding what he was getting into. Determined never to repeat the same mistake, Arian threw himself into learning. He read every book he could find on investing, studied the strategies of successful investors, and began building a foundation of knowledge.

Slowly, he started to rebuild. And this time, he was smarter about it. He did not chase after risky tips or shortcuts. Instead, he focused on simple, time-tested strategies that made sense. By his early 20s, Arian had turned things around. Through patience and discipline, he grew his investments to six figures. That success allowed him to make his next big move: real estate. With the money he had earned, he was able to buy property, using his knowledge and hard work to create real, lasting wealth.

Looking back, Arian's early failure was the best thing that could have happened to him. It taught him the value of resilience, discipline, and never giving up, lessons that would guide him for the rest of his life.

Arian started investing as soon as he could. He was able to understand the basics of the stock market and how to break it down into concepts that would make sense. Arian got so good at understanding this that he was able to teach the content of the Enriched Academy course by the age of 20. Talk about incredible.

And this kid did not come from a family with money. He did not come from an inheritance or have years of schooling. If you ask Arian how he did in high school? His answer would be "not very good at all." Arian and I used to discuss the fact that I was in my mid-30s, completing my MBA while working and having kids. He said he used to struggle in high school let alone the thought of post-secondary education. There I was, on my third stint at university.

The interesting piece here is that he recognized the power of understanding money. The concept of investing principles in the stock market and real estate. The power of compounding interest and how it could work for you significantly. And in some cases, WAY better than my third university degree.

As with any other skills, you need to be open to learning the core concepts. You need to be open to finding time to make it a priority. Most of all, you need to be honest with yourself about your skills and habits (good or bad), and be REAL with yourself concerning what you know, what you do not know and also be open to redefining some of the existing skills to learn how to create better habits and reposition yourself for success.

REFLECTION QUESTIONS WORKSHEET

1. Do you find yourself speaking negatively or positively about your money situation?

2. Do you surround yourself with those who are positive money characters? Or negative?

3. When you are doing a money task – what is your mood? Positive, negative, indifferent?

4. What money myth impacts you?

5. What are you mindful of when it comes to misconceptions about your money?

6. What is your excuse statement? The one you use to justify your spending.

7. Reflect on how the thought of more money impacts your narrative.

KEY TAKEAWAYS

-   Seeking more and more money will not solve your money problems

-   The skill of managing money is more important

-   Learning the skill of saving and investing is similar to learning a language

-   Money does not have to be that difficult if you are open to learning new skills

CHAPTER 3
MONEY MYTHS PART 2

"Do the best you can until you know better.
Then, when you know better, do better."
– Maya Angelou

Continuing with some misconceptions that impact us with our money narrative, in this section we will discuss two that stop us from making changes:

1. It's too late for me and

2. I do not have enough time

As we progress through these two myths, ask yourself:

- Do I find myself using either of them as an excuse?

- Are there any other myths that impact you and your money narrative?

Myth # 3 – It's Too Late for Me

This myth is interesting because, as adults, we tend to think that if we do not know something, it's too late for us to learn it.

This is so interesting. Because if you look at some of the greats who made a splash in their fields such Colonel Sanders KFC, Judge Judy, Vera Wang, Julia Child and even Hollywood 's sweetheart, Betty White - they did not get their start until much later in life.

Colonel Sanders started KFC at the age of 40

Judge Judy started her TV show at 52

Vera Wang started designing wedding dresses at 40

Julia Child started her cooking show 38

And the late great, Betty White did not get her spot on Mary Tyler Moore's show until the age of 51.

I had the pleasure of doing my TEDx Talk alongside Helen Hirsch Spence, who talks about the longevity mindset. Helen's view about life and the lack of appreciation for aging with a longevity mindset is so moving and outstanding. She focuses on how "generations aging isn't a countdown; it's a count up to unparalleled value and wisdom as we adopt a longevity mindset. One that acknowledges that we have longer lives today; we have the chance to reframe the narrative of aging to be filled with possibilities, promise and self-discovery..." The reason I bring up Helen's talk and perspective is it so encapsulates the very myth we are trying to bust here.

If you think it's too late for you, change your mindset. That is your brain and your narrative telling you that. The power to change your view and consider today as the new day to learn the skill of money is within you.

Now, I'm going to give you a real example. Bets was participating in a pilot program for her organization to offer financial wellness for their employees. Bets had worked in the same industry, healthcare, for 30+ years. She spent her career helping other people. When we talked, we had addressed her questions about logging in and how to use a specific tool. I found her questions quite normal for someone who in her generation may not have found technology to be the easiest thing to use. There is naturally going to be a learning curve for her.

After ensuring the technical issues were resolved, I started asking Bets what her financial goals were. I shared that I would be happy to connect her with one of the coaches on the team to gain some feedback for the pilot. To me, this was a win-win. Build a solid case study to help highlight the positives of this program for the employer, through the lens of the employee.

Here's the thing, I had guessed that retirement planning would be high up on the priority list. Given her presumed age, the full head of white hair, and the length of her career, I assumed retirement could not be far around the corner. But that's the thing about assumptions, as Bucky used to say, "They make an ass out of you and me."

Bets stopped fiddling with the tool I showed her how to use and looked at me blankly, "Heather, I will never be able to retire." My stomach dropped or more accurately went into my throat. For those who know me, stumbling over my words does not happen too often nor do I often lack a quick-witted response. I had to reposition myself, give Bets my full attention, and ask some probing questions, "Why do you say this?"

Bets shared that her and her husband had lost money on two homes over the last 20-30 years. They barely seem to have enough to get by every month. So, continuing to work is the only option for them.

Now, I worked in medical education for 10 years, and I know the level of commitment everyone in healthcare made during COVID-19. I looked at this woman and the thought that went through my head at that moment was how in the world could such a kind giving soul feel so powerless about retirement? Her financial stress was so significant, more than anything else in her life. More than holding patients while they're taking their last breath. More than preparing families for palliative care for their loved ones. My heart sank.

We tend to have these pivotal moments in our lives when it just hits you like a ton of bricks - that you are exactly where you need to be at a certain moment. That was one of those for me.

I had only met Bets through email up until that time. But what I realized was she had been suffering in silence. I guarantee if you were to ask her managers, colleagues, etc., none of them would have known the struggle Bets was experiencing on a day-to-day basis.

So, after hearing her story, and the fact that she raised her children the best she could, her husband and she decided they would continue to put their heads down and show up every day.

I had made the decision at that moment to have her paired with one of our financial coaches for a basic evaluation of her situation. Behind the scenes, I had requested the assigned coach to give her as much assistance as needed at no cost. However, "do not tell Bets" was my only instruction. If she seemed like she wanted more help and was committed to doing the work, then let her know we were giving it to her.

A couple of months later, I got a sincere thank you for the generous gift the team had bestowed on her. Even more rewarding is that she was able to create a retirement strategy that would lead to being mortgage-free and being able to retire within 11 months.

Bets shared the following with me after finishing her plan: "I do not even have the words to convey what this gift has meant to me. Aside from my children, it is the best gift I have ever received. First time I've ever felt in 'control' of my finances. It has been life-changing." Everytime I re-read that quote, I still feel the pool of tears in the corners of my eyes.

Bets did not think she would ever be able to make a change, and retirement was so far out of reach. But this is the power of recognizing your mindset is everything. Especially when it comes to our money.

It is never too late to make adjustments. Now that's not to say that your strategy will not be different based on your age. You may be in a position where you have to be more conservative, you may need to do some aggressive debt reduction strategies, or you may need to add a year to your plan. Ultimately, you are going to be in a position to make whatever change is necessary so -that the amount of time you have will be maximized.

Self-Reflection Questions

1. What's your excuse for not getting started with managing your money?
2. Do you think you cannot learn?
3. Any other reason you haven't started?

Myth # 4 – I Do Not Have Enough Time

Sam Huff's famous quote is "We all get 24 hours a day.... It's up to us as to what we do with those 24 hours." This quote resonates with me a lot for this myth. Now, for this chapter, I will be putting aside the controversy around this quote because Beyoncé's life is different from mine, and I acknowledge that. But for this concept, I am still going to rely on the fundamentals of this saying.

We make choices when it comes to our day. The time we get out of bed, outfits, breakfast or no breakfast, coffee or tea (let's get real, there's only one choice there), our choice of driving to work, taking public transportation, you get my drift. Now some people would say, hey Heather, if I had more money like in the first myth, then I'd be able to afford more things to free up more time. But I'm not letting you sink back into that mindset. Because we know now that's a temporary solution.

You need to commit some time to your financial well-being. Only you can make the choice to say yes - these matter to me and I am going to carve out X number of minutes per day, X number of minutes per week, X number of minutes per month, whatever it is. That is within your control.

Trust me, many people always ask me, "Heather, how did you manage to work full-time, run a business, have two young kids, a (now ex) husband, and play Ringette, all the while completing your MBA?" My typical joke response was "I'm superwoman, of course, do you not see my cape?"

Truth be told, I made a lot of concessions, some interesting choices in my diet, and way too much coffee, but I knew I could do it. Why was this? Because it mattered to me. I wanted those three stupid letters behind my name so that I did not have a glass ceiling above me when it came to my career. I made it a priority.

This is why it matters for you to think about where you can make your financial wellness a priority. Start small:

1. Instead of scrolling through reels, could you look at your budget for 10 minutes?

2. Can you update your net worth tracker for 15 minutes a month?

3. Can you add in some financial goals for yourself? Realistic ones? (We will go into this a little bit later).

4. What is in your way to make this a priority?

That last one is a big one. I am a big believer that our money narrative is influenced by the history of our families. Generally, our parent's patterns with money influenced us. Typically, you see three things:

1. a household that talked about money,

2. a household that fought about money, or

3. a household that avoided money

Those narratives influenced you. Think about your parents, your guardians, and the house you grew up in.

Was money a sore spot?

Were there arguments about money? Misalignments?

The common phrase "Do not tell your father/mother I bought this" was passed down too many of us without us realizing its impact. I laugh at that statement now, but I'm not going to lie, it did happen in my home from time to time, too. But it was usually my mom buying something for one of us girls who did not want to hear anything about it from her husband. So if you are influenced by your family's money narrative, of course, you need to stop and think to yourself, "Hey, does this impact me?"

Where did my family fall in that spectrum; am I doing the same things?

It is sometimes a positive thing – but remember – most of our parents were not formally taught how to manage their money either, so I say stop and start reflecting if that influenced you – good or bad. And be aware of that.

Going back to the concept of making time for this, it ultimately comes down to you. You carve out time and make it a priority.

I remember having my first daughter, Tenley, who I swore did not learn to sleep until she was two and a half years old. Basic tasks such as taking a shower or eating breakfast seemed too difficult to commit to. But for some reason, staying on top of my finances was the easier one for me.

Keeping track of my budget and money gave me a sense of control over what seemed to be such a chaotic time. Maybe it was the fact that my salary was only 50% of what it would have been if I was working or that I was running a business with my ex-husband, and at the time controlling something such as my finances seemed so much easier than managing a little human.

Some people are born with the parenting gene. I, on the other hand, had to learn it and earn it. Sometimes I still question whether I got there, but the interesting part as I faced motherhood, head-on, with varying opinions on what I should be doing with food, sleep, and everything else that comes with parenting - that was harder than committing the time to make my money work for me.

Now, for some of you, it will be the opposite. You may find solace in reading Dr. Seuss or Berenstein Bears 100 times over with a smile on your face, watching the same Disney movie over and over again until you can recite it in your sleep. Yet the concept of budgeting or money management makes you want to vomit. So, you avoid it or push it away until it becomes an issue that you have to deal with.

So, let's think about this. Think about your resistance to making money management a priority.

Reflection Questions

Do you know what is blocking you?

Is it time?

Is it an emotional reaction?

Is it feeling inadequate?

Or do you feel you have it under control?

Regardless of what you answered to those questions, I truly believe as the teachings of Enriched Academy and other financial literacy training goes, we are generally on our own.

This is why I want you to dig deep here. If you can set a goal for work, set a goal for your kids' future i.e. putting money away into a RESP, if you can get in the car and drive yourself to work, you can remember to shower or bathe or whatever it is, THEN you can commit to improving your financial wellness. I am giving you permission to make it a priority; now give yourself that same consent.

Think about one area or time in your day or week that you can say, "I will start with 15 minutes." That's it. Start small.

As soon as you have that time carved out, put it in your calendar. Friday morning at 9 AM I will start my budget, I will update my Net Worth tracker, review a video on how to do X, log into my bank account, and start seeing where my money is going.

The cool thing is that, as soon as you pick one thing and add it to your weekly calendar for 15 minutes, all of a sudden it becomes more of a priority. But here's the caveat, no cancelling that time block. That is where the slip happens.

Have you ever tried to add a workout to your calendar during the day? Like right before lunch or after lunch? And it's the first thing to go?

We've almost all been there - myself included. So, this is where making time for yourself and your financial wellness is in your own hands. Find a time that you will commit to. Also, be mindful that if your happy time is at 9 PM watching TV, **DO NOT** put it in that slot. You are just setting yourself up to hate that time.

If you are one of those people whose employers offer financial wellness, take advantage of that. I love working with companies that offer financial wellness. That was my role at Enriched Academy: working with organizations in implementing financial wellness for their employees or members. And when you have a company committed to building a culture of financial wellness, they will allow you 15 minutes in your workday to work toward this goal.

So, pick a time you do not have any other meetings, that will not impact your deliverables, and plop into your weekly calendar. That will be the commitment you make yourself to get the ball rolling.

REFLECTION QUESTIONS WORKSHEET

Myth 3:

1. What's your excuse for not getting started with managing your money?

2. Any other reason you haven't started?

Myth 4:

1. Do you know what is blocking you?

2. Is it actually time?

3. Is it an emotional reaction?

4. Is it feeling inadequate?

5. Or do you feel you have it under control?

6. Where can I put the time to commit:

7. What specific task am I committing to:

Key Takeaways

- It is never too late. You can learn the new skill of managing money at any time, any age.

- You own your calendar. You can make financial wellness a priority by making it a priority for yourself.

- It does not take a HUGE commitment. Starting small will have a big impact.

CHAPTER 4
WHY FINANCIAL WELLNESS MATTERS

"The way to stop financial joyriding is to arrest
the chauffeur, not the automobile."
– Woodrow Wilson

Key Items

- Relationship impacts

- Health impacts

- Trauma responses and other items we may not know

- Work impacts

The Meat and Potatoes

I am not going to lie - this chapter gets me excited to write about. This is the why part! Now, if anyone has ever read Simon Sinek's "It Starts with Why," you might know how that concept resonates. So, as we go through this chapter, I want you to find the piece of the WHY that is relatable for you. Pick the moment/driving force to be the kick in your butt to make financial wellness matter for yourself.

This is the funny part of this concept: you are the driver. You can choose what road to take, what exit to get off at, and when you want to slam on the brakes. I am empowering you in this section to use whatever catalyst you want to connect to in the examples I'm going to highlight. Whatever helps you get yourself on the path of financial wellness.

In this chapter, I am going to highlight the fundamental areas in which the lack of financial wellness impacts us the most. These areas are in our relationships, health, work and even trauma responses.

Money Narrative and Relationships

We spoke about in the last chapter how our family situation affects our money narrative. Now we are going to take it a step further and highlight how it affects our relationships.

According to recent statistics, the divorce rate is sitting at about 52%, and what I have learned working with police and first responders across Canada is the divorce rate goes up to about 60-70% in those industries. So, the batting average for a lot of marriages is not the best.

While I do not think money is the only contributing factor to a relationship dissolving, we do know that it does have a significant impact on relationships. And it is argued to be one of the top contributing factors to conflict within a marriage. Some statistics we have found state that 42% of divorces are due to financial problems, that is almost half.

In my TEDx Talk, I use the example of the saver versus the spender in the relationship. The saver is the one putting money away for a rainy day, while the spender is piling up Amazon Prime boxes at the door, desperately trying to break down those boxes before the saver gets home. Now some of you are giggling, as that example is very relatable.

If Amazon Prime is not used in your household, I am sure there is something you and your partner have conflicting perspectives on when it comes to spending money. In my marriage, my ex-husband used to criticize me every time a new pair of shoes showed up on the doorstep. But when I think about it, it was anything I bought that he believed to be a non-necessity that caused strife.

However, I did our budgeting, I knew how much I could spend on my Amazon prime and shoe purchases because I had put the money away. Yet, he could go and buy God knows what John Deere tractor, tool for the backyard, or Stihl product that does something or other that I still do not understand and expected me to just a suck it up, regardless of the cost.

Or the time that building a chicken coop was supposed to cost $500, only for me to come home to a chicken mansion that I swear probably cost closer to $5,000. But hey, who was I to judge, right? Buying children's clothes or pull-ups via Amazon Prime or organizational baskets. There was also this one time that I came home from a work trip to a giant hole in the backyard the size of an Olympic skating rink that cost more than our kids' post-secondary school savings account. I guess it depends on who you ask and what the hole was going to be used for but projects do run over budget, remember, Heather (p.s. that line makes me so itchy).

At the end of the day, our issues came down to more than just money. But that is a whole other story we are not going into today. I will share that having discussions about each other's spending was difficult, uncomfortable, and generally heated. And we did well financially. So, the interesting thing for those of you in relationships: having money conversations can sometimes boil down to the fact that it really does not matter how much you have, the true issues come when you are not on the same page as your partner. And that is what's stressful.

Think about some of the money contentions you have in your household.

Self-Reflection Questions

What are they about?
Are there specific themes?
Are there specific stressors?

We discussed that the household you grew up in influenced your money narrative. If you are not mindful of that narrative, you will 100% be bringing that into your relationship. Ask yourself, did your household fight about money, avoid it, or get on the same page about it? Whatever the answer is, there is a good chance you take the same approach in your relationship. Otherwise, you may be the rebel without a cause; try to do the opposite.

Then think about your partner. Imagine if their narrative was opposite to yours. And you have never spoken about it. This could be one of the reasons why you and your partner are struggling.

When it comes to money in relationships, we generally recommend making it a priority to work together and start talking about these basic concepts. If you can open the dialogue here, or consider working with a money coach to help you, thinking and reflecting on your styles together will make it easier when it comes to real decisions.

If you find out your spouse is opposite to you, then finding the time and space to have the conversation about money that works for the both of you is important. For example, your partner just got home from work, maybe had a rough day. There is a good chance that is not the best time to start talking about big budgeting items or the fact that you had to spend more on the credit card. Maybe you can find a time that you both agree on, before turning on your favourite TV show and pouring the glass of wine or tea, to start reviewing things together.

This one small step demonstrates that you're agreeing to make money the priority in the conversation during that time. Maybe for you both at the beginning, you'll have to do it once a week. Then maybe once you start working on your goals and strategies and coming up with your plan, you can go down to once a month. Ultimately, it depends on where you're at when it comes to your money situation and how much you want to work on making it a priority. We're going to talk about where you are in your money situation in the next chapter.

Money and our Health

There was a study completed by the Financial Consumer Agency of Canada (FCAC) that digs into the health impacts of lack of financial wellness (as I mentioned previously) but highlights some key points. Here is what they found:

- In 2019, 42% of people claimed to have lost sleep over financial stress

- Financial stress is the number one impact of stress

- 40% of working Canadians feel overwhelmed by their level of debt

- 48% say they've lost sleep because of financial worries

- 35% spend all of their net pay or even more

- 44% say it would be difficult to meet their financial obligations if their pay was late

- 37% say they will have to delay retirement because they will not have enough money saved

They continue to share that, those who suffer from financial stress are:

- twice as likely to report poor overall health

- 4 times as likely to suffer from sleep problems, headaches and other illnesses

And that financial stress can also lead to more serious health problems, such as:

- heart disease

- high blood pressure

- depression and anxiety

More recent studies highlight that since COVID-19, those numbers have gone up to over 72%. Almost ¾ of us are stressed about money, and that stress has a significant impact on us as individuals. We stress over money more than our own relationships and personal health.

I know what it's like dealing with health and the stress around that. I was diagnosed with having precancerous cells back in 2019 when I was pregnant with my second daughter.

At that time, it was precancerous so I was not too worried. Fast-forward to 2021 when I am at the doctor's office every six months, holding my breath to see whether it turned to cancer – now that experience was stressful. My head spun with questions about whether I'm going to have enough money put away to support my kids, being a sole proprietor with no benefits, and how if I do not work, I do not make money.

We had just bought an expensive home that we saw as a long-term investment, but when you are going through health stuff and you worry more about whether or not you have a tomorrow, or you question what tomorrow's going to bring - a long-term investment strategy does not feel comforting.

So, I found myself looking for alternative healthcare. A big question to myself was should I pay for private surgery? Should I pay for disability insurance? Should I pay for benefits in case I need chemo drugs, or anything that may come in case it turns into cancer? Should I get critical illness insurance? Will I even be approved?

Some people do not think about those things, and they only think about their health. But doing what I do for a living, I would be a hypocrite if I did not start looking at those questions.

Most people do not have the means to be able to pay for private healthcare; they wait for the system to get them in and hope that they get the spot they need early enough.

I am a huge advocate for looking for alternatives in case plan A does not work. In my case, there was a two-year waiting list for surgery, I had just received a living inheritance from my mom after my stepdad passed, and I was not sure why I was holding onto that money. But paying for my surgery quickly bumped up on the priority list more than anything else for my financial goals.

Now I'm lucky, I was able to have surgery via a fantastic doctor (thank you, Dr. Singh) and I am forever grateful to that man and my supportive scheduling angel (VH – you know who you are). Because, boy, am I ever happy that I did. Post-surgery, he called me after getting the results, saying that the cells had turned to cancer and that if I had not advocated to move to surgery up, I would probably need to go through additional treatments.

I tell you this story for two reasons: we think about the impacts of financial stress on our health usually when it's too late. If you're not making your financial wellness a priority, you are hurting your health. And secondly, if you are dealing with health issues already, that is stressful enough.

I want nothing more than you to have a plan and a strategy in place for your money so that you can just heal. So you can concentrate on what matters, getting better. And not have to worry about whether you can afford medication, the time off, alternative care, etc.

Trauma Response and Money Narrative

Digging into our health a little deeper, one area that is generally misunderstood is the impact that trauma has on our money narrative. I have worked most of my career to date in medical education and I learned about the impacts of post-traumatic stress disorder (PTSD) on overspending. I was also able to see some similarities when I started working with police organizations and first responders. The "risky" behaviours started to appear as a common thread with some struggling in debt.

When I dug into the research, it appeared that PTSD was linked to overspending because of the dopamine boost that occurs. Dopamine is that temporary mood booster that pretty well eliminates feelings of sadness and stress. People get that kick of dopamine from various reasons: food, working out, sex, drugs, alcohol, and sometimes even social interactions (for all you extroverts reading this).

However, our brain is wired to crave these boosts. Hence why people struggle with overeating, overconsuming, working out too much, or even craving sexual release. Sometimes we feel that dopamine is a rewarding feeling.

So, if you are suffering from previous trauma and you have been ensuring that you are finding healthy ways to get your dopamine boosts, you still might be overlooking a certain area: shopping. Whether we are doing a "smallenfreuden," micro-swipes, tap-and-gos, or even large buys – we get dopamine boosts. Therefore, we can find ourselves self-soothing without even knowing it, with a very easy-to-get-out-of-hand coping mechanism.

Now, as someone who has suffered her fair share of trauma, I will say that retail therapy is definitely something that I have had to learn to manage over the years. Mine were not big purchase items, but I will tell you that filling my shoe rack was the area that contributed the most to my dopamine boosts. And in all honesty, I still get the biggest smile putting on a new pair of kicks or nice stilettos. But over the years, when you come to recognize your patterns of when you buy, how you buy, and what you buy, you start to be more mindful that just because you are having a rough day at work, buying a new pair of shoes may not be the solution.

A good friend of mine is a former paramedic who shared with me that she would find herself racking up her credit card after a "bad call" day. Unconsciously, she would find herself at Lululemon or another clothing store throwing down hundreds on new outfits or something, when in reality she could not afford it. When we had this conversation over dinner about the correlation between PTSD and overspending, her jaw fell on the floor. She finally had the lightbulb moment for herself.

Now, I want you to reflect for a minute and ask yourself whether you have any purchasing habits to help with your mood.

Money Narrative Reflection

Do you find yourself looking at the Canadian Tire magazine for the next sale?

Looking at new cars? Going grocery shopping?

Once you start to note your habits and patterns, you can start to see the impacts on you and how you can begin to rewrite that narrative.

Money and the Workplace

Changing gears a little bit, we're going to start talking about the impacts of financial wellness or lack thereof in the workplace. This is where I geek out.

In my MBA paper, I researched the impacts of an employer-sponsored financial literacy program on employees. Professionally, I was running our division at Enriched Academy implementing financial wellness for Canadian corporations and associations. I wanted concrete data to build on the anecdotal work we were doing to help validate it. I had experienced so many positive stories from employees sharing their personal successes and the effect that their learning had on them that I wanted to bring some academic clout to what we were trying to do.

The FCAC had done their research as I mentioned, and other organizations like the Conference Board of Canada and Ivey Business School, supported by a financial institution, had continued to do their research as well. The funny thing: they were all talking about these variables that impact employees, but there was no consistency, and it did not seem like it was measured appropriately. So, I took it upon myself to find the answer. Well, not completely on my own. Obviously with the support of Enriched Academy and my professor, Dr Scott Rankin, we started asking some big questions.

Here's what we found: regardless of income, employees are stressed about money at all levels. Regardless of self-declared skill in managing their money, employees were stressed about it.

The FCAC and Canadian Payroll Association stated that on average 42% of employees admitted to spending about 3.5 hours dealing with money issues while at work. So, if we look at this. That's a cost to the business. If you start applying simple math to this, based on the number of employees and the amount they get paid, suddenly that's a significant cost to the organization in lost productivity.

My research supported this notion. However, I could also see it was hard to track. And given the statistics to date and the change in the workforce post-Covid, those numbers significantly increased.

We also saw that commitment to the organization was increased by employees who claimed to be less stressed about money. The commitment scales used demonstrated a correlation of clustering, some fancy statistical term, that pretty much says people who are receiving financial literacy from their employers may benefit, which results in them being more committed to the organization overall.

Now there were other arguments claiming that absenteeism increases due to financial stress employees are suffering. However, we were unable to prove this, but what we were able to see were signs of people showing up to work dealing with money issues, which results in presenteeism. This is a fancy HR term, meaning people are showing up to work but being distracted. They would rather be there instead of taking the time to deal with their personal financial issues because it would look bad. Or they could not afford to take the day off.

All in all, financial wellness matters because if we are provided with an opportunity to manage our money issues at work with a resource that's approved and can help us, we're going to be more productive. We also are going to be working in a culture that supports us managing money, thereby building a culture of financial wellness. And when we're given that opportunity by our employer, we're generally grateful.

This is why I argue that we are better humans overall when we're committed to dealing with making financial wellness a priority. We're better in our relationships, we're healthier, and we're better employees.

Reflection Moment

I want you to pause and reflect on this section to see where the impact of financial wellness is impacting your life.

- Relationship

- Health

- Work

- Others

Depending on what you respond to, I want you to select one area where you can rewrite your narrative.

If it is in your relationship, maybe you can start the dialogue about money narratives with your partner. Ask them what theirs is. If they know?

If it is your health being impacted, maybe you can carve out time in your day, week, or month to make your commitment to your overall health by managing your finances. Similar to how people put a "workout" block in the calendar, maybe you can put a financial health block in yours.

When it comes to work, maybe you can discuss with your employer about looking into some financial wellness programming. I may know someone who can help that discussion with you.

Are there any other aspects of your wellness you feel are impacted by your finances?

This is where you can dig in and start looking at your life and stressors. If money is high up on that list, continuing to the next few chapters will give you some tangible focus areas.

Key Takeaways

- Money stress impacts our relationships and workplace.

- Overspending and trauma are linked; be wary of the impacts.

- You can discuss financial wellness programming with your employer.

CHAPTER 5
WHERE AM I AT?

"Life isn't about waiting for the storm to pass;
it's about learning to dance in the rain.
It's about removing the fear in this area of
your life so you can focus on what matters most."
— Tony Robbins

In this chapter, we will discuss an important concept that determines where YOU are with your money. It comes down to four buckets: in debt, living paycheque to paycheque, saving and investing, or doing quite well financially.

We will dig into each of these buckets in-depth, and as we do, I want you to be honest with yourself and start to pay attention to your reactions to them.

Think to yourself

1. Do I even know where I am?

2. Do I fall into multiple buckets?

3. Am I being honest with my situation?

4. Do I have a plan/strategy to move forward?

With over 20 years' experience in business and working with thousands of Canadians, Enriched Academy has determined that we fall into one of four buckets when it comes to our money. Understanding these buckets and where you fall is critically important as we approach the next couple of chapters on what you should be doing next.

The Tough Buckets but not Forever Buckets

The first two buckets are living in debt and paycheque to paycheque. These two buckets make up half of us, regardless of our income level. Again, it does not matter how much money you make, ½ the population are living in these buckets.

So, if you are here, first of all, I want you to remember you are not alone. Kevin Cochran reminds us during his training that this does not have to be a life sentence either. I mention this important point because when we are living in debt, it can definitely impact our mindset.

We feel the weight of it, assuming we are mindful of our debt, or we feel stressed and at times feel stuck. Stuck in the thought that we will never get out or stuck fixating about the way out of it.

In many discussions with people in debt, they admit that even though they know "what they need to do" to get out of it and it should be "easy," things do not change. For many of us, it is a lot harder to reach. There is no shame in being honest with yourself. Because remember, we were not formally taught how to manage our money, so you were on your own trying to figure it out.

I thought this would be a good time to discuss what living in debt actually means. In this particular case, it would be carrying consumer debt (credit cards or lines of credit) or living with student loans (which can be considered a good debt for some).

For this book, I do not consider a mortgage a debt to be worried about, if you are not overleveraged. What do I mean by overleveraged? Well, Enriched Academy spent a lot of time conceptualising what a good amount of money is to spend on our housing, and anything around 30% or less of your total income for your housing costs is what we should be aiming for. We will cover this in more detail in the next chapter though.

Therefore, if you are struggling with credit cards, line of credit debt, personal loans, or student loan debt, that is what I would define as living in debt.

When we are looking at living paycheque to paycheque, here is the example I want you to think about:

Month One:

- You get your first paycheque of the month, you pay all your bills, and you have nothing left.

- You get paid your second paycheque, you pay all your bills, and you have nothing left.

Month Two:

- You get your first paycheque of the month, you pay all your bills, and you have nothing left

Wait – LIFE HAPPENS!

- Your tire blows

- You have a hole in your roof

- Your furnace stops working

- Your kids' sports registration is due

So instead of preparing for this ahead of time, you lean on your credit card, your line of credit, or the very small amount of savings you have.

Does this sound familiar?

What if it is a big cost? You find yourself carrying that debt month-over-month, until you can pay it off.

This is the living paycheque-to-paycheque mentality. And this is stressful because when you finally get yourself out of that hole, you get hit with something that life throws your way and get knocked back down.

This is the vicious cycle that too many of us stay in. Obviously, with half of us living this way, no wonder financial stress is impacting our day-to-day lives. Because in all honesty, we cannot control those life curve balls – they generally come hard, fast, and out of nowhere. And if we do not have the basic fundamental skills built up to manage our money, we will, unfortunately, stay in that mindset.

As I mentioned earlier, in the section about money myths, this is where we get stuck in the narrative of "if I only had more money, I would be better off. These issues would not be a problem because I would have the money for them." BUT – I am going to stop you there. We are moving away from that.Reflection Moment

Self-Reflection Questions

Think about yourself currently:
Do you resonate with either of these buckets?

   a. If not, jump to the next buckets.
   b. If yes, then I want you to stay here a bit longer.

I want you to reflect on some of the money narratives or issues that you have right now. Here are some guiding questions:

- If I am in debt, what is preventing me from paying it off?

- I feel I have other bills that come first

- I continue to overspend every month, and I never have enough to pay the minimum or just above

- I am not sure why. When I think about it, I continue to go out for dinner and buy Amazon Prime products regularly, and the debt sits there

- I have been able to pay it off, but the example of life resonates with me. Life is getting in the way that causes me to slip back into debt. However, when I am not dealing with "life extra stuff" I feel I can manage my debt

If I am living-paycheque-to-paycheque, what is preventing me from preparing for "life curveballs":

- I barely have enough at the end of the month to put away

- Other "things" come up every month that I do not put money away for life events

- I like my lifestyle, and I do not want to put money away for things that do not matter right now

YOLO Living anyone? You only live once mentality – this is not the answer to your spending habits. As the guys (Kevin Cochran and Jay Seabrook) usually share, if you are saying this sentence when you are about to purchase something – STOP. This is one of the most expensive sentences you can say other than "I WANT A DIVORCE." Which by the way, I am ok with. Choosing happiness and health over sticking it out in a marriage is ok by me. Why, because we can help you rebuild – but that is a whole other chapter on its own (stay tuned for the Bonus Chapter at the end of the book).

In the next chapter, when we discuss "What do I do now," we will talk about some strategies that you can take to help you. But for now, we are going to jump into the other buckets. Feel free to jump ahead at this point. Unless you want to read on and highlight some key points for you in the longer term.

The Next TWO Buckets

For those of you who are Saving and Investing or self-declared Doing Great Financially, we typically see a couple of areas of concern here.

Firstly, because we were not formerly taught how to manage our money, we were informed about our strategy by either managing it ourselves or "figuring it out." We went through some rough learning moments that taught us what NOT to do, or maybe we were educated through financial institutions, advisors, mentors, or others in our life to help us make some informed decisions.

Maybe you are one of those types of people who tend to read, staying on top of financial education books and just geeking out with this stuff. Whatever your reasons are, it comes down to the fact that you have TAUGHT yourself, unless you are a Certified Financial Planner (CFP) or Financial Coach, both of whom I do not expect to be digging into this book too hard – unless you have clients you want to recommend it to as a starting point.

So, the neat part here is, even though you are doing some things correctly, I can almost guarantee you have opportunities to learn and refine your practices to do one or two things even better. This was honestly where my ex-husband and I had the most opportunity to learn.

We were doing quite well financially, having a rental property, a primary residence, savings for emergencies, savings for retirement, and investments for our children's futures, plus savings for a $10,000 per year trip to Disney that we paid for in cash. So, all and all, we were doing well for our age.

But the biggest takeaway for us was the opportunity to dig into our investing style, our types of investments, our diversification strategies, and our retirement lifestyles and financial goals. I will say, this led to a lot of very heated, uncomfortable conversations. And while we made significant income together plus our business income on top of our salaries and his commissions, my old self would say that money should have never been stressful. But it was.

It was difficult to broach conversations because his parents fought about money constantly, and the "old school" male narrative that he used to carry versus my hyper-independent strong woman mentality really clashed at times. Not just with money – but for a lot of things in our relationship. Hence, it was a big reason for our divorce. I will not dig in too deep here, but I can honestly say upon reflection that we did not trust each other well when it came to money. Regardless of how transparent either of us was, we were not aligned.

I want you to start thinking about your opportunities to learn here. I want you to think about areas for improvement.

Reflection Moment

- Do I know my investment style?
  - » Does it accurately reflect the right amount of time I have to invest?
  - » Does it accurately reflect the risk level I should be considering?
- Do I know the fees I am paying regarding these investments?
  - » Management Expense Ratios (MER)
  - » Deferred Sales Charges (DSC)
  - » Discount Broker Fees
  - » Brokerage Commissions
  - » Fees for service
  - » Trading fees or commissions
  - » Sales charges (front-end load/initial)
- Do I understand how these fees impact my returns?
- Am I diversified enough in my portfolio that if something dips, I will be ok?
- Have I considered my investing strategy to include key accounts such as the RRSP/TFSA in Canada?
- Am I utilizing my spousal options, if married?
- Am I aware of all the investing options available to me?
- Have I considered looking into alternatives such as real estate?
- Have I considered self-directed investments?

While these are only some of the questions to begin asking yourself, you can see there is a lot to cover here. Interestingly, there does not exist a "one size fits all" when it comes to these buckets.

The biggest impact Enriched Academy sees all too often is the investment fees. This one focus area is a big opportunity for most individuals. Why? Well let's run through an example that the gents use in their training:

They were working with a client who had inherited some money from a family member. Let's call this guy Tim. Tim was working with a financial advisor at his bank who had provided an estimate of taking the initial investment of $200,000 to approximately $1.1M after 30 years with approximately an 8% return and 3% MER fee.

Given the MER fee, Tim remembered that you could ask questions about this, and looked at alternative portfolios or even alternative advisors before investing. Therefore, Tim took the time and did this. He looked at the options that resulted in him investing the money with a different portfolio with only 1.2% MER Fees. This small adjustment resulted in the projections for the return to be similar, around 8%, and after 30 years, he was projected to have closer to $1.99M. This exercise put close to $900K back into Tim's pocket with very little effort. It came down to knowing what questions to ask and learning about how the fees associated with these investments do matter in the long run.

For the visual learnings, here is the example that Kevin
Cochran put together so you can see the impact of
understanding those fees.

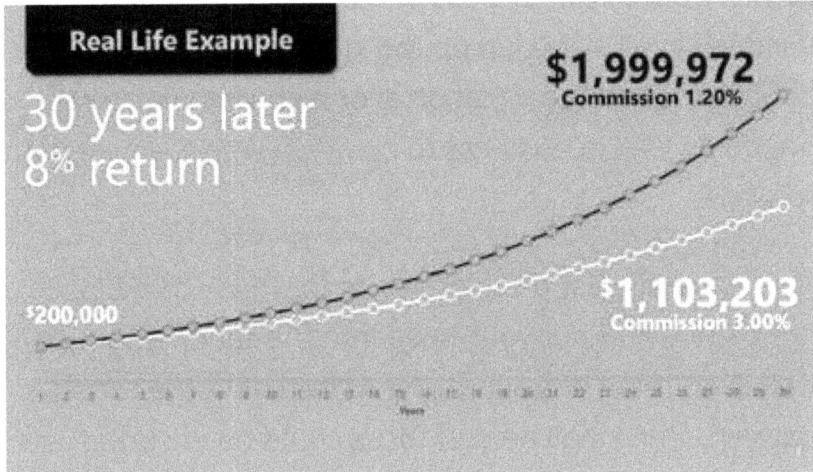

Real Life Example

30 years later
8% return

$1,999,972
Commission 1.20%

$200,000

$1,103,203
Commission 3.00%

© Kevin Cochran, Enriched Academy's investment training section.

The important part here is just because you are
doing well financially does not mean you do not have
opportunities to refine and maximize your situation.
You must be honest and willing to dig into what you are
doing. This is where some of the money myths impact
this group the most – not having enough time. Because
things are not in dire straits, we can easily push learning
to the side, such as improving our habits or looking
for more ways to invest our money, or even validating
that the strategies we have employed are the best path
forward.

Sometimes, you need to be willing and open with yourself to understand that there may be better ways to get to the results you want. One of my favourite quotes comes from a former boss of mine, Dr. Viren Naik, who used to say, "Let's open up the kimono" and be honest about how bad the situation is or highlight where we are doing well in business to come up with the best path forward.

This is the biggest piece of advice for these buckets: do not ostrich and put your head into the sand, assuming that everything is gravy, baby. As we know, life can happen. One small area of focus could be ensuring you are prepared for those life factors and protect your assets.

We do know that a simple task such as having a Will, Powers of Attorneys, and other pieces of your Estate Plan in place would be one of those important things to do for your overall financial wellness, but many of our narratives get in the way here.

Enriched Academy partnered with Canadian Legal Wills, whose entire premise is to teach Canadians how to put a basic will in place, what it means to be in the role of an executor, and what is involved in other important roles such as powers of attorneys (POAs) etc.

From this partnership, I had the pleasure of traveling all over Canada and teaching the material to thousands of Canadians. The one thing that stuck with me during this training is how over 60% of individuals do not have a will. Of those who do, many are out-of-date (which typically means that they are not representing your estate or wishes accurately).

This is another area we tend to turn a blind eye to. We generally do not want to talk about the idea of us dying or not being here one day. And listen, I get that death can make people feel uncomfortable, yet when it comes to your money, you have to get your head out of the sand on this one. We will all die one day. And a Will is our plan for our hard-earned assets.

A question I want you to ask yourself if you do not have a Will right now:

Self-Reflection Questions

1. Do you earn an income? If Yes, you need a Will.

2. Are you over 18? If Yes, you need a Will.

3. Do you have any assets? If yes, you need a Will.

    a. An asset does not have to be big – but if you have a pet, a car, a dresser in your room – whatever, it is best to plan what you want to happen to those items (precious or not).

Many people forget some of the intangible assets that they do not see, such as their pension or retirement savings. Whether small or large, these have value. And even if you are single, child-free, or without anyone you could think of at the top of your head who could benefit from this, it is worth giving some thought and formalizing it.

So, while I am not going into the depths of Wills and Powers of Attorney for this book, I am saying this could be an area in which to learn and educate yourself to ensure that you are taking care of some of the aspects of your financial wellness that you have built.

That is the point in this chapter: once you can acknowledge honestly where you are at, we can start planning for the path forward. And while the roads we take may be different, including when to exit, when to turn, and when to PIVOT (enter the Ross Meme here), we should start to see where we are on that map. Because to figure out where to go and how to navigate the road, we need to start being honest with ourselves, so we can get out of our way.

REFLECTION QUESTIONS WORKSHEET

1. Which Bucket am I in?

2. If I am in debt, what is preventing me from paying it off?

   - I feel I have other bills that come first

   - I continue to overspend every month, and I never have enough to pay the minimum or just above

   - I am not sure why. When I think about it, I continue to go out for dinner and buy Amazon Prime products regularly, and the debt sits there.

   - I have been able to pay it off, but the example of life resonates with me. Life is getting in the way that causes me to slip back into debt. However, when I am not dealing with "life extra stuff," I feel I can manage my debt.

3. If I am living -paycheque-to-paycheque, what is preventing me from preparing for "life curveballs":

   - I barely have enough at the end of the month to put away

   - Other "things" come up every month that I do not put money away for life events

   - I like my lifestyle, and I do not want to put money away for things that do not matter right now

4. If I am saving/investing, do I know the fees I am paying?

5. Do I have a Will?

6. Am I diversified enough?

Key Takeaways

- Knowing which bucket you are in with your money helps you make a plan for next steps.

- Everyone can learn some new strategies to manage your money.

- You do not have to be ashamed of where you are because you have the power to change it.

- Half of us are living in debt or paycheque to paycheque, and remember this does not have to be a life sentence.

CHAPTER 6
WHAT DO I DO NOW?

"Money has no inherent value; it's what we do
with it that matters"
- David Chilton, The Wealthy Barber

Key Concepts

- Net Worth Tracking

- Budgeting

In this chapter, we will discuss the two fundamental
steps you SHOULD do now to take that first step in
making your financial wellness a priority:

1. Net worth tracking and

2. Budgeting

If you are doing both things already, stop and give yourself a pat on the back.

If you are doing one of the two, stop and give yourself a pat on the back.

If you are doing neither, stop and pat yourself on the back to commit to doing so moving forward.

Net Worth Tracking

As Rob Berger, contributor to Forbes magazine, so eloquently puts it: "Net worth is the single most important financial metric one can track." He continues to share that "it represents the sum total of your entire financial life, reduced to a few numbers." The best way I can articulate net worth tracking is consider it your report card for your money. This is the ongoing step you take to view where you are at with your money.

Numbers do not lie at the end of the day. So, unless you are lying about what numbers you input into your Net Worth Tracker (NWT) then the results will be the real deal. Piece of advice - do not lie to yourself. Use this statement and exercise to be honest. Remember, there is no shame in where you are at currently because the only way you can improve where you are is to take this step.

I recommend Net Worth Tracking as the first step for three reasons:

1. Because you need to see the numbers to be able to set your strategy

2. Because if you decide to work with 1:1 support, this will be a requirement for you anyways, and most importantly

3. This could be the **ONE** commitment you can make to yourself now.

This first step to making your financial wellness a priority will be the first goal you set for yourself. This goal is to update your NWT on a monthly basis as a commitment to your financial wellness.

Both Jay Seabrook and I have taught this topic to so many people across Canada with differing financial situations, and regardless of what bucket you fall into, it is the one area that everyone can commit to doing or doing more consistently.

What is Net Worth Tracking?

This comes down to tallying up your Total Assets – things you OWN against your Total Liabilities – things that you OWE.

You can google a Net Worth Tracker statement but the reason I love the Net Worth Tracker Enriched Academy created is how it includes other key items such as Net Passive Income, Net Passive Expenses, and Credit Utilization. I will discuss these terms in more detail as we go.

The total assets are on the left-hand side of the sheet and your total liabilities on the right. For the visual learners, look at an example in the accompanying workbook available at www.heathercoleman.ca)

Listen, the first time you complete this task it will take longer, about an hour or so depending on whether you have access to all the information and it is readily available. The information you will need includes your bank statements, investment account statements, pension details, mortgage statements, loan details, etc.

Your total assets will include items such as:

- Deposit accounts (chequing, savings)

- Investment accounts, pensions

- Properties

- Other assets including vehicles, jewelry of significance, art collectibles etc. or anything that has significant value. Do not bother including furniture or anything like that.

If you decide to read my bonus chapter, you will quickly learn my opinion on stuff being stuff, and the value of those depreciating assets are next to nothing. Moving on....

Your total liabilities will include items such as:

- Credit cards

- Lines of credits

- Personal loans

- Mortgages

- Other liabilities

The major factor here is you want to include the balance of what you OWE on them. However, if you pay your credit card balances off every month, you still want to list it but place a zero beside the balance owing.

Your Net Worth will be your total assets minus your total liabilities. That is it. When you start to visually see this number, you can start seeing the goals you want to set for yourself. I want you to be mindful of your narrative of why you cannot make this exercise a priority for yourself. If you cannot think of one, I want you to pick a day of the month where you are going to commit to updating it every month.

For me, I pick the 15th day of every month at 9:00 AM while I am having my morning coffee. That is my small commitment that I can make to myself every month that takes about 15 minutes. It is also during this time that I reflect on my goal for the month. I write it on my NWT and I follow up with myself the following month. Whatever your goal is, you have a better chance at achieving it by writing it down. We will dig into this further next chapter.

I can confirm that if you make this a priority for yourself on a monthly basis, this small exercise does make you more accountable for where you are with your money. And I guarantee you scroll reels more than 15 minutes per month. So I want you to **STOP** right now and put your calendar reminder in your phone to do your NWT monthly. I'm giving you the minute to actually do it. I am not continuing until the next page – take advantage of this time and space.

Now, to circle back to the other terms I noted earlier, let us start with Passive Income and Passive Expenses.

Passive income is the money we make in our sleep from our investments. This is where understanding your return on investment numbers will come in handy. The interest you make off your money is passive income. Passive income is what we are striving to increase over time versus our active income. When I say active income, I am referring to us trading our time for money ie. going to work, side hustles, etc.

While making more income can help, you do not want to be working forever, thus getting in the mindset to start growing our passive income allows us to continue to grow our money without adding more energy. Do you know the statement "work smarter, not harder"? This is a perfect example of that.

Passive expenses work the opposite way of passive income. It is the cost of borrowing such as the interest rates we pay on our mortgages or loans (credit cards, lines of credit, student debt, etc.). The amount of passive expenses is subtracted from our passive income, and we are left with the Net Passive Income.

This is a number we want to see increase over time and is one of those key metrics to pay attention to on your journey to making financial wellness a priority.

Credit Utilization is one of those other key metrics to pay attention to. Many of us are not even aware of this number, and it is one of the factors that affects our credit score. It is the amount of credit we are using out of the total available credit available to us. Think about your number now.

What is the total amount of:

- Credit cards

- Lines of credit

- Mortgage

- Home equity lines of credit

- Etc.

Now what is the balance you are using of that credit?

Let's say the total amount of credit you have available to you is $100,000 and you are using $30,000. You would take 30,000/100,000, which means you are using 0.3 or 30%.

Now, anything above 30% utilization impacts your credit score. The other factors impacting your credit score are your credit history (how long you have had credit) and credit payment history. Also knowing that if you have a hard credit check too often, that can impact us as well. So be aware of that. However, soft checks (let using a company like credit karma or transunion to stay apprised to your credit score) DO NOT impact your credit score and we highly recommend that you have access to these options as part of staying on top of your financial situation.

When you are thinking about getting rid of your oldest credit card from when you were 18 – stop! Remember it has the longest history. Whether you are evaluating your credit cards and points, you can keep an old one. If you do not trust yourself with it, put it in the freezer, reduce the available credit, or speak to a financial coach for more personalized strategies. However, eliminating it could lower your credit score very rapidly.

Before moving on to the next strategy, I want to recap why net worth tracking is worth it:

1. It is easy to do

2. It allows you to set goals

3. It allows you to see where you are at

4. It tracks multiple factors that you need to pay attention to

One of the best quotes here is Peter Drucker's "You cannot manage what you do not measure." Therefore, using this tool allows you to measure your financial report card.

Budgeting

The second important step you can take for yourself is having a budget, sticking to it, and evaluating whether you are staying on track.

The purpose of a budget really ensures you are living below or within your means. That you are not overleveraging by spending more than you make. However, for half of us, we are overleveraging because recent statistics are showing we are spending $1.75 for every dollar we make. Our grandparents had a very different tactic, spending maybe $0.75 for every $1 they made. Some even less than that. I am not going to go deep into inflation and how our lives are more expensive now, because yes, I get it, we do spend a lot more on life now than they did. However, I also know that we OVERSPEND on EVERYTHING more than they ever did.

Globalization was almost non-existent back then. I know many boomers share stories of certain fruits and vegetables never being known to them as kids because they were from another country. Yet here we can get strawberries almost any month of the year even though it's minus 35 degrees outside. My thoughts here are that we can reset our mindset a bit to be more aligned with the save more, spend later mentality that previous generations did so well.

With that said, I know some people's narratives around the word budget are a real thing. I remember one lady who said it made her itchy to be told she needed a budget. Her David Rose facial expressions were undeniable. She said, "I work hard for my money, and I should be able to spend it how I like without feeling limited." Now this is such an interesting notion because a budget puts you in the driver's seat of spending your money and puts more control into your hands about how much you have to spend on discretionary things aka the little pleasures.

If the word makes you itchy, then rename it. One of the coaches at Enriched Academy shared a neat perspective that I have shared with many people who struggle with the budgeting concept: Spending plan.

Do you like to spend money? Yes! Then make a plan to spend your money!!

It is the same thing, but if it helps you from getting out of your own way, let's go with it.

In this section, I must give most of the credit to my friend, Alanna Abramsky, the Founder of Broad Money and a Financial Money coach. I thought I was a budgeting queen until I met the best of the best, Alanna.

Her story is pretty neat; she wrote a blog about her experience with budgeting when she was living in Toronto, earning a net income of $50,000 (after-tax income), and she was able to save $20,000 in one year to travel part of the world with her friends. Her budgeting style to make it happen came down to knowing what she was spending, knowing where she could be successful at trimming down, and setting a goal to reach it. You can read more about Alanna's story at www.broadmoney.ca

The budgeting or spending plan starts with these five things:

1. Using a budget tool

2. Start with your Net Income and Pay Yourself First

3. Track your Fixed, Variable and Irregular Expenses and Calculate your overall spending

4. Set your monthly goals to reduce spending

5. Continue this quarterly or annually

We are going to go through steps 2-5 in more detail but starting with step 1, the question I get too often is "What budget tool should I use?" The answer is whatever you will ACTUALLY use. Enriched Academy offers three different tools to support their learners. What it comes down to is: can you use it and will you use it?

I personally use an Excel spreadsheet because that is what I am comfortable with. However, some people use ones connected to their bank accounts. In the end, it does not matter as long as you can do the exercise and continue to use it.

Step 2: Start with your Net Income

Your net income is the take-home amount you bring home after all taxes and deductions. If you are self-employed and if you are not already taking tax off the top, this should be something you consider doing moving forward. Open an account and based on the amount of income you have made in previous years. Aim to take something along the lines of 25-30% (you can always ask your accountant/bookkeeper for more specific numbers for your situation).

If you have a partner/spouse, you can budget together. You take your total amount of Monthly Net Income and include that in your income lines.

You will also want to include any other income you get on a monthly, including:

- Government payments
- Rental income
- Other

You will tally that up and get the amount of money you will be working with.

Now, a question that usually gets asked when training this section is about those who have a pension, "Do I include my pre-pension deductions or after-pension deductions?" Well, we want to concentrate on actual cash flow so you will be using your post-pension amount.

Pay Yourself First

Next, you want to get yourself in the mindset of paying yourself first and putting money into your savings. Now, these numbers will be different for everyone based on the situation you are in. The magic number you want to save will depend on a couple of variables:

- What is the amount you need?

- Is it for the short term or long term?

Some people like to wait until step 4 to put the amount in there. However, the purpose of bringing this section up before expenses is getting into the money narrative of paying your future self first before spending. There is a lot written about putting away 10% - however, that number is arbitrary if you do not do the exercise to decide what you need and want to put away.

Step 3: Tracking Your Expenses

Ok – I am not going to lie; this is the part when we are going to be opening your kimono. You are going to get vulnerable and real with yourself. This is when I need you not to pull away. I need you to dig in.

You are going to get three months of your expenses, your credit card statements, your bank statements, for all accounts.

We are going to get three highlighters or markers. Some people do it on the computer, but I am telling you for the first time you do this exercise to print them if you can. Why am I doing this old school? Because it is very real when you physically highlight the expenses. The hand-to-eye thing makes that accountability piece a bit more tangible.

We are going to start with your Fixed Expenses. Pick one colour and highlight every fixed expense over the three months. Fixed expenses are expenses that do not change month over month. For example:

- Rent or mortgage (depending on your payment options)

- Insurance

- Car payments

- Streaming/cable

- Cell phone (assuming no roaming or additional purchases)

- Subscriptions/memberships

- Childcare

- Education

Now, once you highlight each of those fixed expenses, you are going to also write a note beside them to categorize what they are. You can use the buckets above to help, or there may be others that you have. The reason you are categorizing them is that, when you transpose them into the budget sheet, you want to be able to see where you are spending in each of those categories. This makes it easier to set goals for trimming expenditures later in Step 4.

Once you have highlighted all those fixed expenses, you should see that they cost the same month over month. Therefore, you will put the monthly cost of each of those expenses into your spending plan sheet.

Next, we are going to track our variable expenses. These become a bit more difficult to calculate because they do change month over month. The reason we recommend three months of statements to work with is it gives you a more accurate estimate versus one month.

However, some people like to take it a step further and pull anywhere from 6 to 12 months of statements. I am not going to discourage you from that if you want more specific data. I will also say start small so you can actually get in the habit of expense tracking.

Variable expenses include things such as:

- Heat
- Hydro
- Groceries
- Fuel
- Home repairs/maintenance
- Entertainment
- Clothing
- Dining out

You are going to pick one of the other colours and do the same exercise here. You will highlight and categorize each of these variable expenses. You will have to do some math for this one though.

You are going to add up the total amount of expenses in the three months. Let us do groceries as an example. These numbers are not based on anything, just made up to show you an example:

Month 1 - let us say it looks like this:

- $100
- $700
- $275
- $325

Total = $1,400

Month 2:

- $450
- $350
- $250
- $150

Total = $1,200

Month 3:

- $425
- $375
- $250
- $175

Total = $1,225

The three months total is $3,825. You would then divide that by 3, which would equal $1,275. You would enter that number as your monthly grocery expense on your budget sheet.

You will do the same thing for each of your variable expenses.

The purpose of this exercise is to provide you with a more exact depiction of your true spending versus what we think or feel. Many of us create a budget based on what we think we are spending or what we want to be spending, but once you pull the numbers on what you are actually spending, it looks quite different for some.

This is where the accountability starts and becomes real. Remember, no shame. Do not shame yourself for your past spending choices. You are becoming aware of it so when we approach Step 4, you can make those changes then.

Now, we are going to do the same thing for our irregular expenses. This is the section many people forget about and do not account for. Irregular expenses are those that do not occur all the time. The most common ones being:

- Property taxes

- Sports/camps/annual registration fees

- Birthdays, holidays, and Christmas presents

- Professional fees (legal, accounting)

- Vacations

- Prescription/medical expenses (which could count as variable as well)

The funny thing, last I checked, is that Christmas is about the same time every year, and same with birthdays. They do not seem to move – shocker. But the one thing many of us forget to do is account for those expenses in our budgeting.

I am going to give you two personal stories here. The first is surrounding vacation budgeting. My ex and I used to plan a family trip with our daughters on an annual basis. We made the decision when they were young to do Disney for 7-10 days. If anyone has ever done Disney, it is an experience and is expensive. I consider myself a "frugal traveller," so I would plan an epic trip on a decent budget, but all in all for 10 days, with 4 Disney days, it would cost around 10K. Now I know this is a hefty price tag, but we made it a priority for ourselves. So, every month we would put $415 each away for this trip. That meant we were able to pay for everything in cash. So, with hotel pre-booking, I would use my credit card for the points and pay it off the same day. This mentality allowed us to do the trip almost four years in a row with no credit card debt or debt at all.

The second story is the fact that I have a lot of siblings. There are six girls in total, and we used to plan a dinner for at least four of us every year. Given the birthdays do not seem to change every year, I should consider this as a fixed expense. But we will keep it here for now. So, if I went out for a nice dinner plus a gift 4x, that's once per quarter and close to $150 each time. So, a total of $600 per year means I should be putting $50 per month away ($600/12).

Many of us often forget these expenses, so it's key to create a line on your budget or spending plan that includes some of your priorities. We will dive into priorities a bit further in Step 4. But I bring these two examples up for you to demonstrate the commitments to myself that I made a priority and through my budgeting exercise, I was able to make them happen.

You will add all those averaged expenses as you did with the previous expenses and put them into the budget sheet.

Now, the numbers you put in reflect the actual spending numbers for all your expenses.

Step 4: Track your monthly goals

Now that you have your income and monthly expenses, you are at a place to create goals for yourself.

The mindset narrative that you want to take in setting financial goals is to understand your priorities. Similar to the mindset of losing weight, you need to understand where you can continue to give yourself some of those "treats" that do not send you down a spiral of bad eating.

Kevin Cochran talks about a funny analogy: you can do everything right in 23 hours of the day when it comes to your dieting or making healthy food choices, but that one hour you decide to let loose and crush a box of donuts, it undoes all that hard work.

Now I am of the mindset that it's better to set yourself up for success, and dieting is not for everyone. Trust me – I like cake and will continue to eat cake, just in moderation. When it comes to your money, if you take away all the little things that bring you joy, guess what? You may go on a spending spree for more than you can afford. Therefore, let's dig into the priority topic.

Priorities really do influence our money narratives, and they are very different for each person. So, when you get into thinking about your priorities, we like to use this prioritization exercise:

1. Think of the 3-5 things that bring you joy in a month.

Reflect to yourself on the items that you truly could not live without. Is it:

- Dinner out with your friends

- A bottle of wine

- An evening out

- Starbucks coffee beans

- A gym membership

Whatever those items are, DO NOT CUT THEM! Leave them. Because if you eliminate the items that bring you the most joy, you are more than likely going to have a harder time sticking to your budget or spending plan. Your narrative will be one that you are losing out on the things that matter to you. And guess what starts to creep into your mind? Negative thoughts about the whole process, that you have to give up what brings you joy. Therefore, your mindset will be set to that. We do not want that. We want you to have a more positive mindset that notices the items that you can control and cut where it does not matter.

2. Now think about the 3-5 items based on your spending that do not have much meaning.

- Eating lunch out alone

- Online subscriptions

- Bank fees

- Takeout

Whatever your list is from the above, the items that do not have much meaning, those are the ones you will focus on eliminating. Because they do not bring joy, and sometimes, we are not even aware of some of them. Such as online subscriptions and bank fees, we can start to eliminate or reduce our spending in these areas.

Keep in mind that in this section we are trying to set our goals for our new budget or spending plan; your goals may be to reduce debt, increase savings, or just manage your cash flow better. Therefore, once you have seen where you are spending, where you are overspending, and where you can cut, this is a perfect way to set sights on making changes.

As we mentioned in previous sections, you want to move away from the notion of increasing your income as the only solution – so let's move away from that and concentrate on paying yourself more by reducing your expenses.

We have seen some people be able to shave down spending in each of the different expense categories by $300-$700 per month from this exercise. This resulted in anywhere from $900-$1,200 being returned into their own pockets, just by analyzing their cash flow and spending habits. Now, I am not guaranteeing this level of savings but what I will say is that this can be extremely powerful.

For this section, I thought providing you with a couple of real-life examples could be helpful:

a. Cell Phone Bills

This is one area in which you can ensure your plan matches your usage. Also, if you have no contract or are on a month-to-month option, you could call the retention team from the customer service of your provider and request a reduction.

Now, you may need to do some homework here by comparing plan rates with other companies and different offers so that you can be armed with the greatest resource to make your case – knowledge. Knowledge is power and can help you negotiate a better deal.

b. Online subscriptions

There is nothing wrong with having online subscriptions, but if you are not careful, you can find yourself in a position where you are spending in multiple areas and all of a sudden enter a "spend creep." Sometimes something that starts at $5.99 per month all of a sudden turns to $12.99, and then we find ourselves even further down a hole with multiple subscriptions to multiple services, spending hundreds of dollars month over month.

This is where this spending creep slips in. You are unexpectedly committed to multiple providers of the same service and you are overspending. There are other options such as cloud services with different providers, and we are often spending $5 or $12 a month for each provider that offers the same thing.

Hey – I am not shaming you for wanting to pay extra some months to watch Yellowstone when it's finally released. But you do not have to commit to months and months of overpayments for programs that make up a couple of hours per month. If you are intentional, you can take advantage of the free trials that give you 7, 14, or 30 days of free viewing. Binge those shows within those time frames and then cancel. Sorry but not sorry. There is nothing wrong with that OR paying for one month, watching what you want and then canceling. This is not a marriage to a program or a subscription that you need to keep forever.

My partner and I laugh at his disdain for certain "providers," as he refuses to work with them or purchase from them because of a previous bad customer experience. While I appreciate his disdain, I am also of the mindset that if that provider is offering a temporarily free trial that allows you to watch what you want, then hey, put that moral compass to the side for a moment and take advantage of the trial. Set an alarm or reminder on your phone to cancel the trial before the time has expired so you do not get charged unnecessarily.

c.   Coffee

Hi, my name is Heather, and I am a coffeeholic. I enjoy coffee more than a human probably should. I would say that when I am at home, I probably consume a pot per day. My naturopath and sister/bestie, if they read this, are probably both giving me the high brow right now for that statement, but it is true. I like myself some good coffee. However, I have learned a tip when I go into the office. Instead of pouring myself one to-go mug, pour myself two. Generally, it takes me more than one travel mug to wake up, so if I must head into the office, I have polished off at least one mug halfway through my travels. And then where do I find myself before coming into the office? Either Tim's or Starbucks's drive-thru to get my top-up.

It was my wonderful partner who shared with me about pouring two travel mugs before walking out the door. At this point, I looked at him in complete utter shock. More shocked that the person who works in financial wellness never thought about this tip, and secondly, how brilliant I thought it was. Because I am a coffee girl, and I buy better coffee beans. I enjoy good coffee. Therefore, instead of feeling like I am deprived, I buy myself the good beans from some of my favourite providers and I make myself two travel mugs for the road.

I am sure you have other opportunities to cut down based on your prioritization exercise. However, overall, I can almost guarantee that we are overpaying in both home and car expenses. Because as an entire country in Canada, we tend to overspend in both those areas.

Enriched Academy's premise is that if we can keep your housing costs 30% or below your Net Income, you are doing well. Regarding transportation, that number is 10% or below. Now here is the kicker: that is supposed to include your TOTAL expenditures for those items –

not just rent or mortgage. If you consider your heat, hydro, utilities, maintenance etc., it should be below 30% of your total net income. Therefore, if you can find ways to look at reducing your spending here, that may be a focus for you.

Cars, cars, cars – it is a thing. I am not going to lie that they are a necessity for many. I live in the boondocks so a car is a requirement, as there is no public transportation to help me otherwise. With that said, I love the Enriched Academy training here to help get your head out of the "rat race" for owning a brand new, very expensive, depreciating asset. New cars are crazy because for five minutes they are new and five minutes after driving off the lot, they are used. And cars depreciate (lose their value) significantly within the first year.

I know some people love the new car smell or the warranty that is associated with them. However, I will recommend that you do some analysis on your situation before running to the dealership to buy a new one. Doing an analysis of whether a new, used, or leased vehicle is your best solution is something we do not tend to do. We tend to avoid the work of running the numbers and go ahead with the baseline option we had in mind.

I will share a personal story (yeah, money played a lot in my life and I have no shame to share), my ex wanted a new truck for himself. No, this did not lead to our divorce – do not worry about that, but it was a bone of contention. We had replaced his car years ago with an SUV that could be used for the family, and I had an older 2012 Kia that I had bought for myself. My car was reaching the end of its life 10 years later, so he wanted a truck. He came home with a price tag of a new F150 that honestly was 140K all in. The first thing I did when I saw that.... probably vomit in my mouth for a minute. And in my head thought – are you DUCKING kidding me? Yeah, we both know that no one means to write DUCK ever, unless you are a hunter, or you see a duck on a nature walk.

Anyway, moving back to the story, after I worked through all the words that rhyme with duck in my head for a hot minute, I decided to put my work into practice. I asked him ALL the features, things, and shiny objects he wanted in the truck, and I decided to look in the used car market.

Guess what I found? I found a 3-year-old truck with less than 30K kilometres on it (for anyone outside of Canada, that's not that much in miles) and the cost was 59K. It was a better-trimmed version being the Chevy Silverado High Country. It was bigger, had more towing power, and more importantly, I was able to confirm it only had one owner, and running the background check on it, I learned the previous owner babied it. Took it in for oil changes, all required maintenance, etc. So yeah, we bought the used truck. We were able to transfer the warranty from the previous owner onto it so that it provided peace of mind, and we ran the numbers for insurance and it was not much more than we were currently spending on my old beater. DONE! SOLD!

Some people also need to look at how to pay for a used vehicle because they do not have the cash for it. Here is the thing, you can get quotes for car loans, if needed, not only from the dealer but alternatives such as your bank or other financial institutions. The key here is ensuring that it is an open loan so that if you ever are in the position to pay it off quicker, if you can.

I am not going to harp on you for buying a car. I do want you to take away from this example that taking the time to run the numbers on it does really matter. From deciding if new, used or lease makes the most sense. The payment options, the loan type, etc. Do the work.

Ok now we will move on to Step 5.

The key when it comes to your budgeting and tracking of your numbers is to ensure that you do not make it a one-and-done thing. You want to do this exercise on a quarterly or at least annual basis to ensure that your spending is being accounted for.

You want to commit to yourself that you are budgeting enough for each section of expenses because, depending on the time of year, heating bills may be more expensive, and other items you originally did not account for in the first three months may come up. This way, you can start building on your budget actuals and setting realistic and attainable goals.

I covered a variety of items in this chapter and even threw in some personal rant stories about how budgeting really is a powerful tool you can implement tomorrow. The purpose of this are the key gems below.

The Gems to Take with You

- Start net worth tracking regardless of where you are with your money.
- Budgeting or net worth tracking really are keys for financial wellness. It allows you to live below or within your means, understand your spending habits, and set goals for yourself.

The next step is for you to carve out the time and energy to build these into your habits. I am not asking you for hours among hours to add these into your lives. Net worth tracking will be 15 minutes per month once you get it set up. Your budgeting exercise may be an hour per quarter after you do the first heavy lift. All in all, these commitments really do make a difference for your long-term success.

If you have been paying attention to your money narrative around these two steps, hopefully, you can start moving into a positive mindset around why these two steps matter, how they can make a difference, and how you can actually carve out the time to make an impact on your financial wellness.

Reflection Area

1. What Budget Tool will I use?

2. Do I find the idea of budgeting an issue for my money narrative?

3. Can I improve my budgeting strategy?

4. Do I net worth track?

5. What tool will I be using to net worth track?

6. When will I start my budget?

7. When will I start net worth tracking?

Key Takeaways

- Net Worth Tracking is the first commitment you will make to your financial wellness.

- Budgeting works, end of story, so you need to make it a priority.

- You can take the steps to make both a priority for yourself and your financial wellness.

CHAPTER 7
UNDERSTANDING IT ISN'T THE SAME PLAYBOOK FOR ALL - AND THAT'S OK

"The only person you should try to be better than
is the person you were yesterday."
— Tony Robbins

Key concepts

- Rapid fire tips

  » Getting out of debt

  » Retirement planning

  » Understanding your own financial goals

- Start to act

In this section, we are going to conclude the book. I made the conscious decision not to go down the route of all things money. I wanted to focus on the money narrative pieces that get in our way regardless of where we are with our money. As you start your path forward on making Financial Wellness a priority, what I need you to remember is that your path will be different than others, and that is ok.

We all have different relationships with money and our own narratives are as unique as our own fingerprints. Thus, no two people will take the same path. There will be options you will be comfortable with and others are going to be a HARD NO. The most important thing I want you to take away is making some sort of pathway forward. You cannot get stuck in the current mindset. You need to commit to yourself whether it is something small such as learning to know where you fall with your money, coming up with a financial goal for yourself, or learning something new such as self-directed investing, real estate, or even managing your cash flow better. Whatever your choice is, it is totally up to you. But I want you to make that commitment to yourself.

However, I thought I would wrap up by answering some questions that continuously get asked of many of us who present on these topics. As it seems, there are always those rapid-fire questions when I do a presentation that is consistent regardless of the group I present to. So, I thought I would get ahead of those burning questions and give some rapid-fire tips. Here it goes:

Should I pay off High-Interest Debt and/or Save Money?

This one is always a doozy and to be honest there are differing opinions on it. The one notion I want you to remember is numbers do not lie. So, using them to your advantage can help you with your strategy here. With that said, it does not hurt to work 1:1 with an expert to ensure that the right financial strategy is in place for you.

If I am saving money and getting a return of 7% and the interest that I am paying on my debt is 12%, guess what is happening? Every month, my net passive income will be less than my net passive expenses as we highlighted in the Net Worth Tracking section. Therefore, if you can pay off your higher-interest debt faster, then you will have a better return overall.

It comes down to math. Higher-interest debt works against your net passive income. Therefore, work to pay it off or reduce the interest rate as soon as possible. Then you can take that money you were paying in debt and put it all towards savings.

Should I be saving for my retirement?

The short answer is YES! Now, if you have high interest debt, pay that off. Then take that money and plop it into your savings. The amount of money you should be saving for retirement comes down to what you will need in retirement. There are some tremendous calculators out there that help you determine if you are on track or need some adjustments to your savings. The key numbers required are:

- Your current age

- The age you plan to retire

- The age you will live to; estimations are fine here (average life expectancy)

- Your current income

- Your estimated income you want in retirement*

- Your current retirement savings

- Any additional income

Once you have these numbers, most calculators will walk you through some basic questions. For any Canadians, will you be receiving OAS or CPP? The numbers will run you an estimation to show you if you are on track.

Now, the key step is the estimated income you want in retirement. Like the spending plan/budget exercise, do the same with what you anticipate your needs will be. We cannot tell the future but you can probably get a sense if you will be mortgage-free, want to travel more, know roughly your food costs, etc. You will run a budget sheet with these estimates, similar to what you did in the previous chapter, to determine your required expenses and work backwards from there.

This will determine the minimum amount you want monthly, and multiply that by 12 – bam, there's your estimated income. Be mindful though that you may need more money towards insurance and healthcare. But many of your other expenses may have decreased.

This retirement planning is key. Because it will help you determine now how much you should be putting away monthly for your retirement savings goals.

Understanding your financial goals

Ok – this one will change over your age and stage through life. One moment you're saving desperately to buy your first house (try to take advantage of all the first-time home buyers' plan options as possible).

Then it shifts

- Maybe you are trying to max out RESP grants for your children.

- Or looking to buy a rental property.

- Or looking to pay for your MBA as a mature student (been there, done that).

- Or looking to maximize your retirement savings to get the biggest tax reductions.

Whatever your goals are, they do pivot and change over time. Life as we all know too well deals us cards that we sometimes do not anticipate. So being able to make changes as necessary to reach the next goal or reset our goals is important.

Many first-time home buyers my age lived through bidding wars for their first homes. I even remember a friend of mine not even looking at the sixth house he bid on because he was so over the hurt every time they lost a bid. Funny enough, that was the one they purchased. Different generations and even different regions face opportunities, draughts, and stalemates that may change your strategy temporarily.

Or in my case, health scares and divorce changed my trajectory. But as with many others I have spoken to, they have bounced back and sometimes even better and further than their earlier paths. I am looking forward to that. Looking back at my price of freedom and now laughing that giving up that lifestyle was the best thing ever.

The purpose of this section is to get in the habit of setting money goals. You are more likely to reach a goal if you write it down. Jay Seabrook is honestly the highest advocate of this, and I have to say he is more committed to his goal card than anyone else I have ever met. The power of our goal-oriented mindsets does pay off. I know there was a famous quote about Sidney Crosby visualizing holding up the Stanley Cup before he finally won. And Jim Carrey wrote himself a cheque for $1M years before he saw that happen. Therefore, I thought of taking this time for us to walk through a simple goal setting exercise that includes helping to build a habit, with a little bit of fun.

The envelope challenge is one I ran this across all clients one year a couple of months before the holidays, in the hope that people get in the mindset of saving the cash before overleveraging.

Here is how it went: if you start with 60 days, create envelopes for each day.

Day 1, put in $1.

Day 2, put in $2,

Day 3, put in $3 and so on until your 60th envelope has $60 put away.

And guess what? After 60 days, you will have saved $1,830.

Now, expand that exercise to a 100-day challenge, and suddenly you will find yourself saving $5,050.

Now, do that a couple of times over a couple of years, and your saving goals start to become more realistic. I could go on and on about how powerful this exercise is. But this ultimately comes down to you!

Believe in yourself and do not be your own worst enemy. Pick a goal that you want to achieve and WRITE IT DOWN.

Throughout this book, we have emphasized the importance of removing obstacles in your path. However, it's equally important for you to believe in your ability to take the necessary actions to achieve your financial wellness goals. The key is to begin somewhere. As we conclude this book, I encourage you to make a commitment to yourself to take action NOW. Make that pledge as soon as you finish reading this book.

I will start by _____

I will measure my success by _____

I will stay accountable by _____

My goal for the next six months is _____

Then put those calendar reminders in your phone.

Give yourself the time to take the additional online modules. Complete your budget exercise. Start net worth tracking. Do something!!

And guess what? If you need help – ask for it. Do not be ashamed. I know so many wonderful money coaches that LOVE to educate. They just want to help the average person do better because helping others learn how to do better with their money is honestly one of the most inspiring things you can do in your career.

There have been many times I have teared up after a training session because of the level of vulnerability that an attendee has shared with me. The rawness of their story. The realness of their pain. And knowing that my 45 minutes inspired them to take action fills my cup beyond anything else.

CONCLUSION

Money is hard for so many people. Especially when we are conditioned not to talk about it, to pretend we have it all figured out, to struggle in silence with our fears or insecurities around it, among other things. I hope this book inspired you to be real with yourself and start having the conversation. Start looking into your own reactions to money. Your money narratives that impact your relationships, your health, and your work. Because in order to get our minds right, we need to get our money right.

Financial stress and the weight of it causes so much tension in our lives. But I do not want you to shy away from this. I want you to start to name it. Start to be mindful of the impacts it has on you. Start to notice where and when money causes you strife in your life and start to find ways where you gain that control back.

I know this book does not provide you with all the answers you need, but it is meant to be that spark. The starting point to make your financial wellness a priority for you. No more waiting until you have more.....time.... money....no more excuses. Change starts today and it starts with you giving yourself the permission to dig in.

So, thank you for taking this time and a bit of a random journey with me. I hope you feel inspired to start looking into your own money narratives and what impacts you.

Regardless of whether you are struggling or doing well, taking away even one "aha" moment is enough for me.

I look forward to you reaching out and hearing about your next steps and goals for yourself. Feel free to download your Financial Wellness Goal card here: www. heathercoleman.ca

It starts with you, right now.

BONUS CHAPTER
DIVORCE AND MONEY

"And so rock bottom became
the solid foundation on which I rebuilt my life."
– J.K. Rowling

Key concepts

- Preparing for separation and divorce

- KNOW YOUR NUMBERS

- What can you afford and be realistic about it

- Be mindful of the time to rebuild

The truth is many of us are impacted by separation and divorce, more than half to be exact. So this bonus chapter is going to give you some considerations from my unique perspective as a former family law clerk, trained family mediator, child of divorce, and divorcee myself.

First and foremost, I know I can come off cavalier at times, but when it comes to this stuff, I know it is hard. From grieving the end of a marriage, the end of a family, financial distress, and, well, just the complete unknown, I get it.

A wave of emotions comes and goes depending on what led you to the end of your marriage. So, I'm not giving you advice on specific legal issues because depending on where you live, it could change, and frankly I am no family lawyer - mind you I have some good referrals. However, some fundamental issues come up regardless of where you are geographically.

First and foremost, you need to know your finances. You need to start gathering it all. This is where also knowing your partner's numbers is also handy. I have horror stories of spouses only finding mountains of debt after separation. One particular lady was a well-established educator who was approaching retirement. She went to pay her daughter's tuition with a credit card which was declined. She did not understand why. When she approached her then husband, he said he would take care of it. At first she was not worried, until she went to pay for something else and it happened again.

She went to the bank herself only to be given a piece of information that changed her life. All joint credit cards were maxed out, same with the mortgage, and a recent application for a second mortgage was underway, all lines of credits maxed. To say the least, the lifestyle she thought they had was a complete and utter lie. Her husband was so overleveraged, he was paying debt with debt. He had kept his spending and habits under wraps. She made over 150K a year herself and she thought her husband made the same. She did not understand how they ended up here.

This is the BIG WAKE UP call – and I tend to be gender neutral most of the time, but this impacts women way more often than men. However, it could happen to anyone. You need to know your financial situation. You need to be able to understand your partner's situation as well. Especially if you are married or have joint anything. Because it could impact you in the long term. Until death due us part or credit card debt does.

From this point forward, you will make a commitment to learn the numbers. It is fine if one spouse defaults as the money manager, but you will start to know where everything is at. And not just once but continuously on a schedule.

This comes into play because just as there is joint ownership of property there is joint ownership of debt. So understanding what that looks like in totality is imperative.

Furthermore, you need the realization that you were once a dual income and going to be a single income moving forward. That is a majour wake-up call for some people as they quickly realize that the "lifestyle" they had in marriage is gone. You need to recognize and prepare to be self-sufficient. Regardless of whether you have entitlement to support, getting a sense of what your budget is and what you can afford is critical. Will you be able to buy a house on your own? Will you have to move? Will you need additional insurance?

Divorce really comes down to separating the assets built up during the marriage, such as:

- Matrimonial home

- All savings

- All debts

- All belongings

Considering the total of it and dividing it equally. Of course, some factors come into play such as children, spousal support (alimony), inheritances, pensions, etc., so the more you know about this stuff before starting to negotiate, the better it is. Remember - knowledge is power. At the end of the day, it will have to be provided anyway.

I would say in most cases I have seen, the majority do not separate overnight. There is generally a leading up to the "day" space between stages. It is here that it would be a good idea to start understanding what you can afford and what you cannot. You also want to be real with yourself and not be house-poor because you want to stay in the matrimonial home. You may need to consider other options to be able to afford the rebuild stage.

Speaking about the rebuilding piece – be patient. Think about how long it took to build up what you had and know that you can start to rebuild post-divorce. In some cases, it may mean re-evaluating your retirement timelines, your vacation goals, etc., but it does not mean it is forever.

The other piece is recognizing that some of the precious objects you collected over the years, well, are not worth a damn thing. The chattel argument is one that I will say quite bluntly is not worth fighting over. A great family lawyer will tell you to resolve that stuff beforehand as much as possible because fighting over the lamp in the living room while spending $500 per hour is just not worth it. You could probably buy a nicer lamp for less.

Pick your battles and choose the things that do matter i.e. your grandma's urn with ashes. At the end of the day, you will not win it all and you will need to concede to others. The price of freedom is a statement to get used to.

When it comes to divorce, having a support team is critical. Someone you can vent to, someone you can lean on potentially for financial support as you transition, someone you can rely on for legal advice (a good lawyer or mediator). Divorce coaching through the process is also a great way to understand what comes next.

I am a strong believer that if you can resolve the majority of your issues before heading to lawyers, that would be great. However, everyone should seek independent legal advice before making any final decisions. I do not believe in fighting for the sake of fighting because ultimately, everyone loses. The bank accounts get drained in legal fees which ultimately hurts the family in the end.

Last but not least, kids are not pawns. They do not need to be brought into the adult breakup. Family dynamic changes do not have to include putting children in the middle. So a quick word of advice, if you are angry at your ex – get help for yourself. Therapy or divorce coaching is no shame. It can really help you move forward through the issues so that you can concentrate on putting kids first through the changes.

Child support is the right of the child NOT the right of the parent. Regardless of how you feel about paying your ex a chunk of change per month, you need to accept that one. Be honest in regard to how much income you make, and same goes for your ex, so that you both can move on with your life. Sometimes we feel bitter or frustrated but we have to pick our battles, and regardless of what happened to end your relationship, hopefully, you can come to a place that puts the children's well-being first.

I kept this chapter short and sweet because separation and divorce come down to some core issues that need to be resolved but a whole bunch of emotional baggage that also needs some addressing too. As someone who has done divorce coaching for several situations including my own, I would be happy to provide a consultation to you to see if divorce coaching would be a fit for you. Having experience in your corner is never a bad thing. https://heathercoleman.ca/services

So, divorce can be hard, but knowing there is life after, and concentrating on rebuilding the life you want with financial goals that align, is a powerful gift to yourself.

ABOUT THE AUTHOR

Heather Coleman, Vice President, or for those who really know her, Queen of Enriched Academy, is a dynamic leader dedicated to fostering financial wellness across varying organizations throughout Canada. She has spent the last four years researching the impacts of Financial Wellness on Employees and empowering individuals to make informed financial decisions while she completed her Masters of Business Administration from Thompson Rivers University. The successful completion of her MBA led to presenting her research, in collaboration with Dr. Scott Rankin, at the ASAC Conference in 2024.

Leading the growth and development of the Associations and Corporations division, Heather actively collaborates with Canadian Companies, guiding them in establishing a robust culture of financial well-being among employees or their respective memberships.

Heather's passion has led her to travel the country engaging thousands of Canadians in breaking the barriers of having real "money talk" without the pressure of having to buy.

Beyond her corporate prowess, Heather is a passionate ringette player, showcasing her commitment to both teamwork and athleticism, and a proud mother of two beautiful girls. Heather's multifaceted approach underscores her commitment to holistic well-being, in the workplace, at home, and on the ice.

Heather also holds a BA in Law and History, and Graduate Certificate in Conflict Resolution from Carleton University. She ran a Legal Support company for 10+ years, works in Medical Education, is a mother of two, and is an avid frenchie mom.

Heather is a National Speaker with her style being best referred to as the "triple R" effect - Raw, Rare, and Real. Her ability to connect with individuals on a difficult topic has allowed her to inspire those to take the first steps in making Financial Wellness a priority.

Reach her at www.heathercoleman.ca

thank you

Thank you for reading my book!

Dear Reader,

Thank you for taking this journey with me and starting to be raw and real with yourself.

I hope it inspires you to start being more mindful of your own money narrative and the impacts that it has on your financial wellness.

I also hope you take the small steps to start making positive changes in your financial literacy that I can guarantee you will not regret.

If I could ask a small favor: if this book resonated with you, or sparked something meaningful, would you consider leaving a positive review on Amazon? Your thoughts could support others looking for the same kick in the tuckus to make the change they need to their own money narratives.

Cheers,
Heather

RESOURCES

1. Enriched Academy (www.enrichedacademy.com)

2. Broad Money (www.broadmoney.ca)

3. Financial Consumer Agency of Canada (https://www.canada.ca/en/financial-consumer-agency.html)

MY GIFT TO YOU

I am so glad you're here!

As my Gift to you, get FREE Access to the Audiobook of Our Money Narrative and other Free Book Bonuses by scanning the QR Code below or visiting www.heathercoleman.ca

www.ingramcontent.com/pod-product-compliance
Lightning Source LLC
Chambersburg PA
CBHW071422210326
41597CB00020B/3620